Create!

A toolkit for creative problem solving
in the not-for-profit sector

Mark Butcher

DIRECTORY OF SOCIAL CHANGE

Published by
Directory of Social Change
24 Stephenson Way
London NW1 2DP
Tel. 08450 77 77 07; Fax 020 7391 4804
E-mail books@dsc.org.uk
www.dsc.org.uk
from whom further copies and a full books catalogue are available.

Directory of Social Change is a Registered Charity no. 800517

First published 2005

ISBN 1 903991 57 9

British Library Cataloguing in Publication Data
A catalogue record for this book is available from the British Library

Cover and text designed by Stephen Strong
Printed and bound by Page Bros., Norwich

Other Directory of Social Change departments in London:
Courses and conferences 08450 77 77 07
Charity Centre 08450 77 77 07
Charityfair 020 7391 4875
Publicity & Web Content 020 7391 4973

Directory of Social Change Northern Office:
Federation House, Hope Street, Liverpool L1 9BW
Courses and conferences 08450 77 77 07
Policy & Research 0151 708 0136

Contents

About the author   v

Acknowledgements   v

About DSC   vi

Foreword   vii

Introduction   1

Step 1: [C]onfirm ... your problem   7

Step 2: [R]isk ... take some   22

Step 3: [E]xpand ... your options   26

Step 4: [A]nalyse ... and choose the best way forward   63

Step 5: [T]hink ... and develop your creative capacity   78

Step 6: [E]ncourage ... others. Build a creativity culture   114

Action plan   126

Further reading   128

Notes and references   130

Dedication

For Joe and Jamie.

About the author

Mark Butcher is a consultant and trainer who specialises in fundraising, strategic planning and helping individuals deliver exceptional performance. He has worked for many national charities and international foundations in over a dozen countries. He has also been a supermarket shelf stacker, a rock singer, a kitchen goods salesman, a community development worker, an arts administrator and on the odd occasion, an advisor to European Royalty. His first book, *Achieve!*, is also published by the Directory of Social Change. For more details of Mark's work see his website at www.markbutcherassociates.co.uk or send him an e-mail at markbutcher@blueyonder.co.uk

Acknowledgements

I have been lucky enough to meet many people over the years who have demonstrated for me how to think positively, creatively and purposefully. I'd like to thank three in particular for the influence they have had on my thinking. They are: Michael Gilfillan, who is not afraid to dream; his brother Paul, who is not afraid of risk; and most of all, my old mate Ken Potter, who has, for almost 30 years, used a singularly sharp mind to bring clarity and insight to my muddy thinking. I'd also like to thank the many individuals and organisations whose creative opportunities and sometimes brilliant solutions have served as examples and case studies to illustrate this book.

About DSC

The Directory of Social Change (DSC) aims to help voluntary and community organisations become more effective. A charity ourselves, we are the leading provider of information and training for the voluntary sector.

We run more than 350 training courses each year as well as conferences, many of which run on an annual basis. We also publish an extensive range of guides, handbooks and CD-ROMs for the voluntary sector, covering subjects such as fundraising, management, communication, finance and law. Our trusts database is available on both a CD-ROM and a subscription website.

Charityfair, the annual three-day conference, events programme and exhibition, is organised by DSC and takes place each spring.

For details of all our activities, and to order publications and book courses, go to www.dsc.org.uk or call 0845 77 77 07.

Foreword

Why a book on 'creativity'?

Ask any manager in the not-for-profit sector for a list of the skills needed for success and you'll probably get something that includes:

➤ Strategic planning

➤ Fundraising

➤ Negotiation

➤ Project management

➤ Team building

➤ Supervision and appraisal

➤ Leadership

➤ Communication

… and so on.

Absolutely – all of these are essential – but only if they are done well. And I believe that a critical – and often ignored – element in the successful application of the above skills is the ability to be creative. Creativity enables you to see beyond the accepted, usual, normal ways of acting and behaving – in order to find a better, more effective or quicker way of achieving the results you need. Creativity will add an extra dimension to the fundamentals, in much the same way that salt will improve the flavour of a meal. This book is the salt, that hopefully can improve the 'flavour' of every other skill you possess!

But do we really need a book to help us? I'd say yes, and the reason is to be found in three challenges faced by not-for-profits. These are 'Growth', 'Standardisation' and 'Complexity'.

1. Growth

In his excellent book *Managing without Profit*, Mike Hudson outlines five key stages in the development of an organisation. These are 'Birth', 'Youth', 'Adulthood', 'Maturity' and 'Decline'. In the Birth stage organisations tend to be dominated by their founders who are entrepreneurial and 'unwilling to be stopped by obstacles'. The organisations have loose structures and tons of energy. As an organisation moves from this first stage through subsequent parts of the life cycle, it becomes increasingly professional, structured, stable and secure. It can also of course become increasingly complacent, inflexible and less energetic. (1)

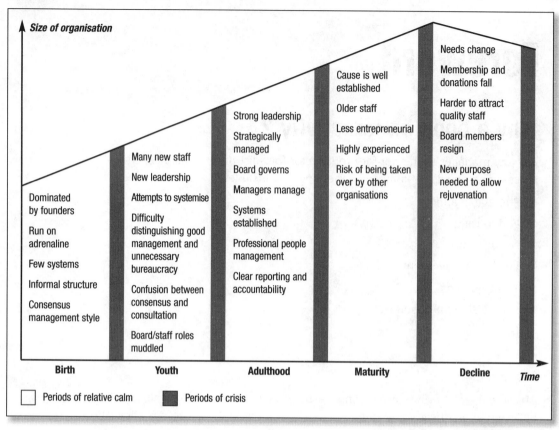

By the time Maturity is reached, organisations sometimes find themselves slipping into the doldrums. Sure, they may be stable, but they're also a bit duller. You will often find old hands looking back during this stage to the 'glory days'. 'Oh yes, we really shook them up back then.' The culture of the organisation becomes less ambitious, less motivational, less able to change. In her book, *Mapping the Mind*, Rita Carter talks of the 'fluid' intelligence enjoyed by children (which enables them to mop up experience and greedily learn new things) and also of the 'crystalline' intelligence that develops as we get older. (2) This enables us to do some things very well, but to adapt and change less easily. You cannot, after all, teach an old dog new tricks. It would seem that the organisational 'brain' goes through much the same sort of development. It is this increasingly entrenched inability to adapt that leads many organisations inexorably towards Decline. This is characterised by increasing difficulty in securing funds for core work, a difficulty in recruiting enough trustees, ever less effectiveness in meeting the most urgent needs. It seems that a growth in stability and a decline in creativity may be inexorably linked – and that in the lifetime of an organisation a critical tipping point is reached where 'same thinking' stops being good and starts to be bad for the organisation.

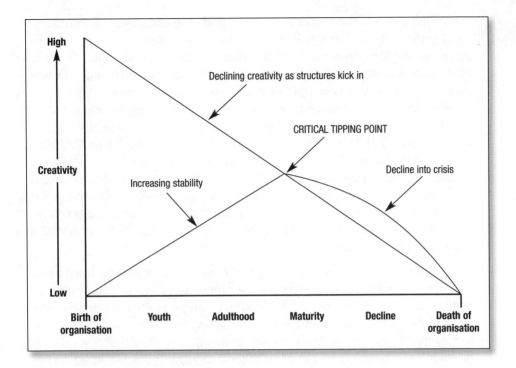

! **As they grow and develop agencies need to be equipped to deal with change.**

2. Standardisation

The last couple of decades have seen a number of interesting trends including:

➤ A move towards greater 'professionalism' from voluntary sector and community bodies.

➤ The adoption of 'best value' quality standards by local authorities.

➤ The widespread adoption of methodologies borrowed from the private sector, especially in areas such as marketing, quality management and strategic planning.

➤ A raft of legislation that impacts on how not-for-profits do business, from charity law, through employment law, to legislation on discrimination and equal opportunities.

Whilst every one of these is to be welcomed in its own right, there is a downside in terms of creativity. Together the above trends represent a standardisation of the culture in which we work. General George S. Patton said 'If everyone is thinking alike, someone isn't thinking'. If emerging voluntary bodies aspire to act a bit more like the established 'big siblings' in the field, if local authorities demand the adoption of established process and procedure in return for a lucrative contract, if a funder as powerful and ubiquitous as the Community Fund imposes its own template of quality standards on so many organisations up and down the land, then it is inevitable that we begin to 'think alike'. There is little doubt that many charities would consider bending their culture to fit with that of a social services department if it led to a valuable contract. An interesting corollary question is 'does this *always* represent the best way to help older people, or children with cerebral palsy, or young offenders?' What if we are all on the same path and it's not the best one? In October 2003 not-for-profit think tank, Centris, published a report called 'The Audit of U.K. Civil Society'. This asserted that in ten years the voluntary sector had massively professionalised, while grass roots participation had declined. Another possible implication of this conclusion is that there is a sweeping trend of standardisation towards commonly accepted models of professional practice running in parallel with a dearth of new ideas emerging from below.

I must stress, I'm not knocking any of the trends or developments listed above. The world is undoubtedly a better place for them. Good work, *great* work gets done within the framework. But we need to be aware of the flip side (*everything* has a flip side) and act to improve further the way we do business. My point is simply that every time an accepted way of doing things become 'beyond question', it becomes harder to bring original thought or creative action to bear.

 There is pressure to standardise. That means there is a risk that we all make the same mistakes at the same time. Organisations need the skills to 'think differently'.

3. Complexity

The more successful you are at meeting need and the better you become at fundraising, the faster your organisation will grow. The faster it grows the more complex it becomes. As the government looks more and more to voluntary sector agencies to deliver its agenda, there is a danger that we will be forever running to catch up with ever-more complex relationships, client needs, organisational challenges and so on.

 Organisations need a creative approach to handle increasing complexity.

The net result of these three key factors is that organisations now face conflicting pressures – to be flexible and able to change, but also to develop systems and structures. Many are also being asked to handle increasing degrees of complexity with increasingly limited resources. Many of the presenting problems, to do with 'strategic planning' or 'mission' or 'personnel' or ' fundraising' or 'team building', I believe are caused by this intractable pressure.

What this book will give you

The purpose of *Create!* is to build the capacity of individuals and work teams to live in this difficult environment and to equip them with the skills that will help them bring alternative, wider dimension thinking to solving the problems described above (you can also use them to help you decide what colour to paint the kitchen!). The book will use the CREATE model (see below) to help you:

> ➤ think clearly about your problems;
> ➤ generate the maximum number of options;
> ➤ think critically to select the best option;
> ➤ develop a creativity culture in your team or organisation;
> ➤ build your own creativity muscles.

Specifically, the CREATE model and the tools contained therein can be used to:

> ➤ help fundraisers come up with new and interesting approaches to securing money;
> ➤ help managers and leaders produce more ambitious, interesting and achievable plans;
> ➤ help facilitators work with groups to solve problems and resolve differences.

How to use this book

The CREATE model represents what I hope is a systematic and holistic programme. I also want this book, however, to be a treasury of ideas to be dipped into whenever fresh inspiration or a new approach to problem solving is needed. The many ideas, tools and methods detailed throughout this book can be applied to a variety of circumstances and situations.

A practical resource to solve problems

I've been helping people in the not-for-profit sector use creative thinking to solve problems for a number of years now. Examples of the kind of concrete challenges that have been solved by applying the tools in this book include:

> ➤ The community law centre which needed to generate new income streams to replace withdrawn local authority funding – and fast!
> ➤ The theatre development officer who needed to get long-term planning on the agenda of a very hands-on but 'short-view'-focused director.
> ➤ The local authority officer who needed to offer the same level of support to community organisations with fewer grants.
> ➤ The drugs advice centre which needed to develop a more cohesive way of working for its various departments.
> ➤ the community centre manager who needed to find ways of dealing with the fact that increased pressure to achieve outcomes, evaluate results and provide detailed information to funding bodies was drawing too much staff time away from the 'real work'.

> The foundation which wanted to re-examine its methodology for selecting project applications and giving its money away.

> A charity doing a wide range of work in Eastern Europe which wanted to re-examine its mission.

Throughout the book I've included many case studies to give you a flavour of how the techniques we cover have been used in practice.

Ground rules

However you choose to use this resource, either reading it from cover to cover or dipping in and out, there are some ground rules which will help you get the most from it.

These are:

1 Bringing originality to a familiar landscape will mean changing that landscape. In the context of creative thinking change is good. But change is also often recognised as being difficult. You might feel uncomfortable with some of the exercises and goals I'll set for you. That's OK, this could just mean that they are working!

2 Some of the ideas in this book should strike you as implausible, ridiculous perhaps even embarrassing. You should feel that I have missed my vocation by spending time writing them down – perhaps you know of a village somewhere nearby in need of an idiot. That also means that we are on the right track.

3 Creativity is no good without the attendant behaviour change. Your behaviour will have to change before you'll see any benefit from the various tools and techniques. You can't get something new *out* if you put the same old stuff *in*.

Sucking something to see is easier than long-term commitment – and that is all I'm asking of you. There is no real risk in trying new ways of thinking. So try to do so with an open mind – in the end you will only adopt the ideas that represent your best options. It is said that the Dalai Lama was once asked by a very deferential interviewer how we might go about changing the world for the better. The interviewer expected an answer resonating with solemn and deep wisdom. His Holiness simply said 'you think about it for a bit, then try something and see if it works'. Now therein is real wisdom!

The six key challenges

You will see as you go through the book that each section ends with a summary and then I set you a challenge. Rising to these challenges will be the key to your ability to improve your creativity and problem-solving skills. There is nothing to worry about – just use the techniques I suggest and you will do it.

Introduction

What do we mean by 'creativity'?

Top management thinker John Adair describes it as the ability to 'open your mind into wide focus to consider all possibilities'. That is, I believe, true – the expansive wide-angle approach to a problem is very important – but I want to go a little further. Consideration on its own is not enough because just thinking about something doesn't actually change anything. To make a difference we need to act on our new way of thinking. For this reason, I like to think of creativity in the following terms:

❗ Changed thinking, leading to changed action.

Habit is the enemy of originality. If we always think along familiar tramlines, then we're not being creative. So clearly, we have to break our habitual ways of thinking (and those of our peers) and find different ones. So far so good. But no amount of different thinking is any good at all if we don't *act* differently as a result. Creative thinking has to lead to new ways of operating, behaving, cooperating and so on. If changed thinking leads to unchanged action, it's a waste of time!

How important is creativity?

Creativity is helpful in our professional and personal lives because it allows us to investigate fully *all* the options of a given situation, before choosing one as the basis for action. A creative approach helps us not just find any solution, but, because we have generated a menu of possibilities and a wide range of ideas, it helps us discover the *best* solution.

This book is about making the most of your gifts, maximising your potential and achieving excellence. Those not-for-profit professionals who can bring an element of creativity to their work enjoy a very special advantage. Because they are more likely to find the best solution, they are more likely to develop a reputation for quality, excellence and action that gets effective results. They will, over the course of a career, solve many more problems more satisfactorily and thoroughly. They will be better at identifying root causes and addressing the heart of a problem, rather than just attacking the symptom. In short, creative professionals and the organisations they work for will be more successful.

The bad news

I believe that there are, however, three main barriers to creativity that prevent us exercising the full power of our creative brain. These I refer to under the following headings:

➤ Precision
➤ Pattern
➤ Position.

Precision (getting it right)

For the best part of two and a half thousand years we have based our thinking in the West on a mode of thinking that classifies, systematises and categorises. The way we think short-circuits creative thinking by giving us ready made 'answers'. The Athenian philosopher Plato first proposed that reality was underpinned by an absolute truth. Things were either 'true' or 'untrue'; there was no middle ground or room for interpretation. His student Aristotle (384–322 BC) built on this to develop and use a principle of systematic logic that meticulously created classifications and categories for fish, bird and mammal species. We live with the conceptual legacy to this day. A chair has to be either precisely 'a chair', or 'not a chair'. But what if I pick it up and throw it onto the fire? Doesn't it then become firewood? What if I pick it up and throw it at you!? Then it becomes a missile, surely? And what if an *Anobium domesticum* was to look at it? Well, to any self respecting woodworm it would appear as 'lunch'.

Nevertheless much of our thinking today is still based on the premise that things are either 'true' or 'untrue', 'right' or 'wrong'. John Paul Sartre referred to what he called 'facticity' – wherein 'facts' are confused with 'truths'. But of course it is possible to interpret facts in a number of ways. I could say I love sport – does that mean I'm probably fit and healthy? Not necessarily, I might just like watching sport. You might say that 'it is cold today'. But if I'm an Inuit Indian I may think that it is positively balmy! It is a fact that you think that it is cold – but there is no *absolute* truth about the matter that relates to *both* of us.

The right versus wrong approach to 'the truth' can be seen clearly in our education system. From an early age children are taught that answers in class are either 'right' or 'wrong'. The late Sir Peter Ustinov used to relate an occasion when he was asked to sit an internal school exam. He was asked to name a Russian composer and answered Rimsky Korsakov. The 'correct' answer was, however, Tchiakovsky! He was upbraided in front of the whole school for 'showing off'. (3)

I think many of us learn at an early age that if you put up your hand and you are wrong, you risk censure, embarrassment, perhaps ridicule from your class mates. It's safer if you don't know the answer to sit on your hands and let someone else take the heat. Because we are taught this approach to thinking when we are young, it stays with us into adulthood, where fear continues to kill a great deal of creativity. When we have a problem with staff morale, disappearing income streams or subtle changes in user need, we sometimes find that fear of getting it 'wrong' prevents us generating ideas, alternatives and options. And this doesn't just apply to professional problems. If we encounter growing debt, relationship problems or worries about our children's behaviour, the need for precision, the desire to 'get it right' and the fear of 'getting it wrong' can prevent the generation of creative solutions and approaches.

 Fear of being wrong kills creativity.

Position

Expressing facts as the one and only truth, and adopting the kind of positional thinking that leads to this kind of expression, is sure to lead to misunderstanding, contradiction, and confrontation.

One is either a libertarian or an authoritarian; new labour or old labour; a feminist or a chauvinist. We buy in to ready-made packages of answers and don't question the assumptions behind them. You put two people in a room from the opposite sides of a spectrum on any issue and you are sure to get fireworks! We see the failure of positional thinking everyday in the mother of parliaments. The government benches take a position. The opposition (almost always) takes the opposite view. Then begins a frantic search to find facts to fit each position, or if there aren't enough facts, to find different ways of interpreting the few facts that do exist. It has always been this way. In 1897 Henry James was writing of the 'fatal futility of fact'.

To find the best solution, it helps to have the ability to question assumptions, challenge the rules and if necessary, break them.

What is the RIGHT answer? How many cubes can you see?

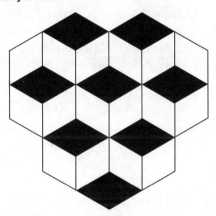

The answer is six. Or it could be seven. Or even 13. It depends how you look at it.

(If you thought you were looking down on the figure from above, with the black panels representing the top side of the cubes, you will have seen seven. If however you thought you were looking at the figure from below, with the black panels representing the underside of the cubes, you will have seen six. If you switched quickly back and forth between each perspective, you'll have seen a total of thirteen.)

! **A need to justify our position kills creativity.**

Pattern

So for much of the time we tend to see things in black and white and argue for our position whenever anyone disagrees. Could it get much worse? You bet! And that is because we are creatures of habit. Habits determine how we eat, drive cars, make decisions, communicate – in fact almost everything we do is the result of a learned sequence of behaviours. Once we have learned to act in a certain way the architecture of our brain is actually remodelled to reinforce repeat behaviour. (4) So every time we decide that something 'just is' and every time we try to back this up with reasoned (?!) argument, we become much more likely to be just as judgemental and inflexible tomorrow. In this way intransigent behaviour patterns start to emerge. These patterns help you to win arguments, but prevent you being open to the alternative point of view.

! **Habit is the antithesis of creativity.**

Some barriers to creativity

Internal	External
Fear: It's risky to come up with ideas in a 'right' or 'wrong' culture.	**A busy environment:** One filled with distractions, noise and interruptions. We'll see later how such an environment can destroy creativity.
Belief: We sometimes think of the 'creative ones' as people who can paint or play the piano, and that we, in comparison, are not creative. But that's just not true. Every time you solve a crossword puzzle, bake a cake or choose an imaginative gift you are being creative. We just need to use the creative parts of the brain more when we are at work. And to do that we need to believe that we are creative and give ourselves permission to have ideas.	**A sterile environment:** Sometimes we experience the same trips to work, attend the same meetings, talk to the same people and read the same papers (not to mention eat the same food, visit the same pubs, watch the same TV) week in and week out. We like the routine. We get comfortable. That feels good – but too much routine can sap the ability to think in new and different ways.
Self-criticism: Be honest – you know that you are your own worst critic!	**Criticism from others:** It's much easier to say 'that'll never work' than it is to say 'let's give it a try'. Many great ideas are the subject of 'infanticide' – squashed before they have a chance to mature and develop.

The good news

Don't get depressed yet! There is actually lots of good news. To begin with, despite everything that has been said, we are all naturally creative. Evolution has developed a fantastically powerful tool for creative problem solving – the human brain. The genes that acted as the blueprint for your brain have been inherited from hundreds of generations of ancestors. Every one of these ancestors was creative enough to survive and prosper in a hostile world, long enough to pass on the gene code to the next generation. The gene strains of those of our ancestors who could not work out how to solve the rampaging wild animal problem, or the fast-approaching drought issue, or the warlike neighbours' challenge, simply died out as the individuals in question were eaten, starved or clubbed to death before they could pass on their low creativity gene codes. Natural selection means that the ability to be creative has been distilled and focused within us all. We are all incredibly creative. Every time you solve a problem at work, make a meal, write a letter or advise a friend you are being creative. Creativity is not the sole preserve of great artists and inventors, we all have it.

More good news

And there is more! Sure, we may have developed bad habits which tend to work against our natural creativity – but we can kick them. The ability to question, think differently, produce lots of ideas from which to choose instead of assuming that the current way is the only right way, to fly in the face of all of the training we have received since childhood, is a skill which can be learned and practised. We do not need to sit on our hands and wait for someone else to provide the answer, we can proactively develop a greater ability to build on our natural gifts and be more creative.

The CREATE programme
– a model for positive creative thinking

The CREATE programme has been developed by Mark Butcher Associates and is based on six key stages. Each one of these stages lends its starting letter to the acronym CREATE. The six stages are:

1 Confirm

If we are unclear as to the exact nature of the problem we are trying to fix, there is always the risk of coming up with the wrong answer. You'll find lots of examples from the private and not-for-profit sectors, as well as from history, in Step 1 of this book. You'll also find a range of techniques for focusing on the right problem and ignoring the 'red herring'.

2 Risk

Thinking in creative ways necessarily means thinking differently from the rest. It means being ahead of the pack, rather than running with it. There is a risk that people will reject your thinking as too radical, or too threatening for them to accept. More importantly, you have probably been trained to think in fairly safe ways, and you may find yourself rejecting your own radical thinking. This book will ask you to leave some of those comfortable, but limiting, behaviours behind. To succeed you will have to lose your fear of failure and become a bit of an ideas daredevil!

3 Expand

You'll need to improve your ability to generate large numbers of ideas. This section of the book will focus on techniques to expand the number of available options, as you search for the best solution to personal and professional problems. The techniques listed in Step 3 of this book are concerned with 'divergent thinking' – the opening out of your mind to encompass lots of possibilities as referred to by John Adair. (5) Divergent thinking is about generating lots of ideas. The key at this stage is to generate, generate, generate. In line with that philosophy, I've tried to give you a range of techniques. You may like some more than others. That's fine. By definition not every idea is a brilliant one – but as we shall soon see, you do need to have a lot of ideas before you can have a brilliant one. Working on that principle, I'm going to give you lots to choose from.

4. Analyse

Once the table is stacked with options, the next sensible step is to filter them, grade them, and focus down on the best ones. Ultimately, the ability to think in an analytical way will help us choose the best idea from all of those generated. This stage is known as 'convergent thinking'. This is the ability to select the most appropriate, effective and workable ideas to provide the best solution.

5 Think

Beyond the step-by-step approach contained in the Confirm, Risk, Expand and Analyse stages, there is also much to be gained by working on the creative process like a muscle. This section of the book will focus on building our personal capacity to think creatively. Like any kind of fitness programme, it is something that needs to be maintained – or we get out of condition. This section of this book is about working on and improving our innate ability to think creatively. It's about being in this business for the long haul.

6 Encourage

There's no point being the sharpest saw in the box if all of the other tools are blunt and rusty. This last section will contain tips and techniques to create a corporate creativity culture within your organisation, to help and encourage team members, colleagues and bosses to support the creativity process and become more creative themselves.

How your mind works – the spectrum of thinking

Your brain has two separate hemispheres – one on the left and one on the right. It is hard to identify exactly how a human brain works – after all it has no moving parts – but nevertheless some techniques such as magnetic resonance imaging have led neurologists to conclude that each hemisphere has distinct properties. The 'left brain' is where logical, rational and sequential thought takes place and the 'right brain' is where intuitive, emotional and associative processes are experienced. This book works on the premise that there is a wide spectrum of appropriate responses to challenging problems based on the different types of thinking that each hemisphere equips us for. Individuals too heavily reliant on either 'right-brain' or 'left-brain' thinking will find it hard to examine problems from a variety of angles and then act appropriately. It has been said that it is an ability to switch between these modes which marks out the truly creative. This toolkit will help you to do just that by offering techniques (within the CREATE programme) that support 'hard' systematic techniques based on the left brain's ability to analyse *and* 'soft' approaches based on the right brain's ability to be intuitive.

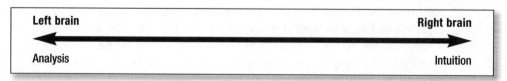

Whether we need to be thinking clearly about the nature of the problem we are trying to solve, coming up with lots of possible options or critically evaluating these, in order to choose the best one, the CREATE programme offers a range of techniques from both sides of the spectrum.

Confirm ...

... your problem

Why 'confirm'?

It goes without saying that if you are confused about the nature of the problem you are trying to address, then you're unlikely to come up with the best solution. You might spent a lot of time privately thinking about the issue and discussing it with colleagues, and you might come up with lots of ideas – but none of these will do you any good unless you are focusing in the right area. This section is about asking the right questions – before we even consider coming up with the right answer.

Section overview

In this section you will:

➤ discover why 'problem' begins with not one, but three Ps

➤ look beyond presenting symptoms, to root causes

➤ use 'hard' left-brain thinking and 'soft' right-brain thinking to identify and record the real issues and challenges you face.

Record your problem

The starting point for this section is that you are not interested in these tools as an academic pursuit, but that you have a real problem (or problems) which need a solution or solutions. The tools in the CREATE programme which we are about to look at will certainly work best if you have a clear picture of the problems to which they are to be applied.

Banker John Pierpont Morgan once said that no problem can be solved until it is reduced to a simple, specific and concrete form. Unless this is so we may find ourselves trying to solve the wrong part of the problem, or even the wrong problem!

The first step in solving a problem is to think actively in order to identify it.

Confirm ...

... your problem

Why 'confirm'?

It goes without saying that if you are confused about the nature of the problem you are trying to address, then you're unlikely to come up with the best solution. You might spent a lot of time privately thinking about the issue and discussing it with colleagues, and you might come up with lots of ideas – but none of these will do you any good unless you are focusing in the right area. This section is about asking the right questions – before we even consider coming up with the right answer.

Section overview

In this section you will:

➤ discover why 'problem' begins with not one, but three Ps

➤ look beyond presenting symptoms, to root causes

➤ use 'hard' left-brain thinking and 'soft' right-brain thinking to identify and record the real issues and challenges you face.

Record your problem

The starting point for this section is that you are not interested in these tools as an academic pursuit, but that you have a real problem (or problems) which need a solution or solutions. The tools in the CREATE programme which we are about to look at will certainly work best if you have a clear picture of the problems to which they are to be applied.

Banker John Pierpont Morgan once said that no problem can be solved until it is reduced to a simple, specific and concrete form. Unless this is so we may find ourselves trying to solve the wrong part of the problem, or even the wrong problem!

The first step in solving a problem is to think actively in order to identify it.

7

Exercise 1

Most of the problems we have to face at work fall into one of the three groups below: The three Ps are **P**eople, **P**rocess and **P**ractice. For example:

People	Process	Practice
Motivating others	Setting up systems	Raising money
Building relationships	Consulting	Finding premises
Changing minds	Gathering information	Managing projects

In the space below, write down a problem that you would like to have solved creatively.

_____

_____

_____

_____

_____

_____

Is this *really* the problem?

A problem well defined is half solved.

John Dewey

Sometimes individuals and organisations fail to make progress because the problem that they think they have is not really the problem at all – they are 'barking up the wrong tree'.

At the end of the nineteenth century a group of German psychologists sought to demonstrate how the brain could be tricked into misinterpreting data to arrive at the wrong conclusion. Look at the two horizontal lines below:

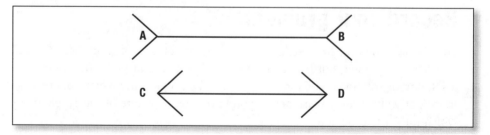

Which is longer, the line A/B or the line C/D? Most people choose the former. However, look closer and you will find that they are exactly the same length. Take out a ruler and check if you don't believe me! This is known as the Muller-Lyer illusion, created by its originators in 1889.

A similar effect was achieved by Edward Titchener in the late 1800s. Which of the two central circles do you think is larger in the figure below?

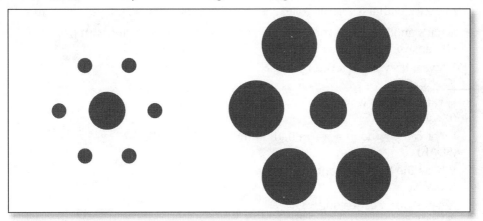

If you chose the one on the left, you're wrong. Once again, they are exactly the same size.

Although these examples relate specifically to visual perception, the mind is just as vulnerable to misinterpretation when it comes to business or interpersonal issues. In fact we constantly misinterpret situations, people and perceived problems. Sometimes we have to ask, 'is the problem as we perceive it the real problem?', because if we focus on the wrong problem, then no amount of creativity will benefit us!

Don't assume

The human brain is great at making sense of reality quickly. The problem is (as the example above illustrates) that it sometimes arrive at a conclusion before all of the evidence is in. There are probably very sound evolutionary reasons for this (if you hear a rustle in the undergrowth – you have to assume that it is a sabre toothed tiger if you want to live long enough to pass on your genes!) – but in terms of keeping an open mind, it might not be that helpful. It's also true to say that we learn from experience. So think about this for a moment …

> we make our minds up quickly

> we learn from experience.

So it follows that when we are faced with a new problem, we will draw on our past experience and use this to decide on the nature of the new problem – even before we've seen the whole picture. Once we've made up our mind in this way, any further evidence is rendered less 'relevant' by the pattern we've established for our thinking.

Case study: It has been said that in the 1960s NASA spent 12 million dollars developing a pen that could write in zero gravity – thus enabling astronauts to make notes in space (conventional pens use gravity to draw the ink to the ball of the nib). A complex, innovative and expensive technology was developed to pump ink, using compressed nitrogen, to the tip of the pen. When it was unveiled, a representative from the Russian space agency rather spoiled the party by asking 'why don't they just do what our cosmonauts do – and use a pencil'! (6) The NASA engineers had assumed, based on their experience of writing, that an ink pen was required.

To demonstrate how good we are at making patterns out of our experience, try this trick with a friend or colleague. Ask them the following questions in turn:

What's another name for a funny story (one syllable – begins with J)?
The answer is of course … (JOKE)

A sweet fizzy drink loved by kids?
(COKE)

What's another word for a boyfriend?
(BLOKE)

What can you do in a warm bath at the end of a hard day?
(SOAK)

What's the long garment that wizards wear?
(CLOAK)

A caress for a cat or dog?
(STROKE)

What do you call the white of an egg ….

I can almost guarantee that they will say 'the yolk'. The white of an egg is called the albumen.

Look beneath the surface

Is your inability to fundraise something to do with the fact that the organisation does not have fundraising skills, or is it that there is a lack of real vision from the board of trustees? (The best fundraiser in the world will fail if the organisation does not have clear objectives and mission).

Is the fact that Sam is on long-term sick leave due to stress something to do with the amount of pressure he is under, or his inability to delegate? If it is the latter, then dealing with the former will create a short-term solution, at best.

Is the health service failing because waiting lists are long, or because clinical priorities are wrong? There's no point in reducing waiting lists if we concentrate on ingrown toenails whilst making the people with early carcinomas wait for a year.

With each of the above examples, it is fair to ask, have the real, fundamental problems been identified, or are assumptions being made, that do not take the whole picture into account?

 If we want to be more creative we have to learn to withhold judgement, keep an open mind and resist the impulse to make assumptions.

Cause or symptom? The '5 Whys' technique

One common mistake people make is to deal with the symptom of a problem, rather than the *root* cause. Remember what we said earlier about making assumptions? Reaching quick conclusions, and closing down our thinking to further options too early may lead us to focus on a problem which is not the real or fundamental problem. For example, if you are under too much pressure at work, you may say 'I need a holiday'. Wouldn't it be better to take the pressure away?

One way of stripping the problem back to its root cause is to ask 'why?' five times. The process works rather like peeling the layers of an onion, like this:

'We need an away day ...'

'Why?'

'Because the staff are demotivated and angry.'

'Why?'

'Because their team leader has just gone on long-term sick for the second time this year.'

'Why?'

'Because he's stressed out.'

'Why?'

'Because he can't cope with the pressure.'

'Why?'

'Because he doesn't get any support from his line manager and hasn't been trained.'

'So what do you need...?'

'AH HA!'

The answer is of course, support and training for the team leader. It's like peeling back the layers of an onion to get to the heart. Why five times? Because it is usually enough. You may find your true problem in two or three. It is rare that you need to ask the question more than five times, but those occasions do exist.

Case study: A trust set up to run a heritage site used the 5 Whys technique to get to the root of a tricky management problem.

Original problem
'We have recently expanded and taken on new staff. Now we find that everyone seems to be stepping on each others' toes. There is no real role clarity in the team.'

Why is that?
'Because we have no job descriptions and no one seems keen to take on the responsibility of writing them.'

Why is that?
'Because the last time we tried, one person in particular simply refused to cooperate. It caused a lot of bad feeling.'

Why is it that the management team couldn't deal with this person's objections in an appropriate way?
'Because we are a flat team, the managers have no real power to manage and this person has used the situation to create a sort of informal power base.'

Before this thinking was gone through, the trust thought that an appropriate solution would be to do more work on roles and responsibilities. Although this was undoubtedly needed for this group of people – the more fundamental problem caused by the non-hierarchical nature of a growing team needed to be addressed first. Unless this issue was dealt with, the trustees realised that they would at best be papering over the cracks by clarifying and defining roles, because no one would 'own' their reclarified responsibilities.

Exercise 2

Try this technique on the problem you thought of in Exercise 1.

Write it down again, then ask 'why?' five times. Write down your new, deeper answer after each 'why?' Stop when you feel that you have reached the core of your problem (this may take less than five questions).

Problem:

_____

_____

Now ask 'why?' five times:
1st 'why?

_____

_____

2nd 'why?'

_____

_____

3rd 'why?

_____

_____

4th 'why?'

_____

_____

5th 'why?'

_____

_____

Did the nature of the problem change? Is there another more fundamental problem to address? Are you now barking up a different tree?

Cause or symptom?
The '3 Cs' technique – how to create pyramid thinking

Pyramid thinking is a way of uncovering the hierarchical structure of the issues within a problem. It works in a similar fashion to the 5 Whys technique, in that it uncovers what (if anything) lies beneath the presenting problem and differentiates between causes and effects.

The 3 Cs technique creates a pyramid, starting with the overall **C**hallenge, identifying key issues or ideas that **C**ontribute to the challenge, and then finally listing possible **C**auses for each contributing factor.

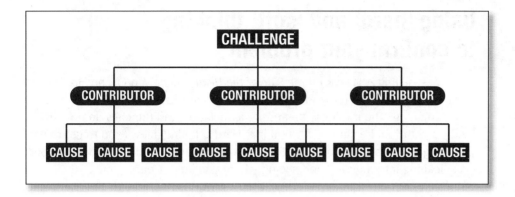

The challenge might be too big or complicated to deal with in a single pass. But if you eliminate the contributing issues that support it then it will collapse. And of course, these will disappear if you eliminate the causes. So get to work on the fundamental causes, rather than focusing on the challenge.

Case study: A Surestart group was concerned that local parents did not seem interested in taking up the services they offered. This was the presenting 'challenge'. After many hours of talking around the problem, soul searching, and many attempts to decide on the best way to proceed, a 3 Cs pyramid was constructed. This identified three key 'Contributors' to the problem, namely, 1. that parents did not 'own' the service, but saw it as imposed; 2. that the staff had been unable to get the message across to parents or to communicate effectively the role of Surestart; and 3. that the staff team were (as a result of 1. and 2.) demotivated and unhappy.

The main causes of 1. were the lack of a mechanism to consult with parents and a lack of effective evaluation procedures.

The main causes of 2. were the absence of decent literature and a reluctance on the part of key staff to get out into the community and 'meet and greet' parents.

The main causes of 3. were seen as a lack of joined-up thinking between the various arms of the service, and the inability of individuals to offer appropriate support to others, because they didn't really understand their colleagues' work.

This thinking led to:

1 Better, and earlier, consultation with parents.

2 The production of a good-looking brochure and training in presentation skills for staff.

3 The development of a buddy system for worker support.

These measures (which were aimed at dealing with 'Causes') effectively eliminated the 'Contributors' and therefore dealt with the presenting 'Challenge'. Parents began to take up services in far greater numbers just a few weeks after the above measures were implemented.

Using 'hard' and 'soft' thinking to confirm your problem

In his best-selling *A Whack on the Side of the Head*, Roger Van Oech calls the linear, sequential, ordered and logical thinking demonstrated by the left brain 'hard' thinking. The intuition, dreaming, association and hunches demonstrated by the right brain he calls 'soft' thinking. Hard thinking allows you to get to where you are going in a series of logical steps. Soft thinking is more like closing your eyes, leaping into the dark and seeing where you land. Neither one of these types of thinking is 'better' than the other. They are both powerful aids to creativity. So long, that is, as you do not exhibit a powerful preference for one sort of thinking at the expense of the other. We need instead, to cultivate a balanced approach.

Using hard thinking to define your problem

As we have seen, woolly thinking can leave us with an ill-defined problem. If that is so, we may be tremendously creative and come up with lots of options, but we will have difficulty selecting the right response.

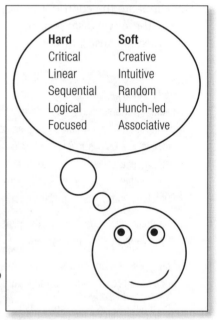

'We need to promote our organisation with the local authority, so we will send every member a copy of our annual report.' Wouldn't it be better to simply build a relationship with the *key officer* who advises the politicians?

'My problem is mounting debt, leading me to seek a better-paid job.' Wouldn't it be better to stay away from clothes and record shops?

'Our problem is that we're having trouble finding funders to help us prolong our project.' Shouldn't you really ask why it is that funders are reluctant to fund the project? Is it well managed? Has it achieved its aims? Has the need it sought to address changed?

Case study: Straight after being told that she had terminal cancer, with three or four months to live, Maggie Keswick Jencks, the pioneer behind the renowned Cancer Caring Centres Trust, was asked by the consultant to move to the corridor because there were so many other patients to see. She wrote 'No patient should be asked, no matter how kindly and how overworked the hospital staff, to sit in a corridor without further inquiry, immediately after hearing they have an estimated three to four months to live'. (7) It is a reasonable point to make. Did the hospital staff see their primary problem that morning as offering appropriate support or getting though the list of appointments? Were they working to solve the right problem?

Three techniques

Here are three more techniques to help you focus down in a logical, systematic way on the issues. These are the Socratic method, the 6 fundamental questions and the fishbone technique.

The Socratic method

The earliest recorded exponent of 'hard' thinking of whom I am aware is Socrates. The Socratic method is about clarifying, clarifying and clarifying some more.

> What do you mean by that?

> Define this term for me?

> Give me examples of what you mean?

> Can you be more specific?

Socrates worked hard to get all of the information in. His approach was based on withholding judgement until he saw every angle. (8) (Take a look at the rabbit opposite. Now turn the page a quarter turn anti-clockwise. See what a new angle can offer!)

The 6 fundamental questions

This technique is today used by professionals who need to get to the truth by digging a little deeper. For example judges and journalists both use what are sometimes referred to as 'the 6 fundamental questions'.

Rudyard Kipling famously said 'I have six honest serving men. They taught me all I knew/ Their names were How? and Why? and 'When? and What? and Where? and Who?' We've already seen the power of 'Why?'. Her brothers and sisters are just as potent.

Fishbone technique

This technique was developed by Professor Kaoru Ishikawa of Tokyo University in the 1960s as a way of comprehensively listing all of the causes or issues that make up a complex problem and separating cause and effect. (9) It gets its name from the fish skeleton it resembles.

It works in five stages:

1   Take a blank sheet and write down your problem in the right hand margin – then circle it. This is the 'head' of the fish and represents the 'effect' of the issues. It is not the root cause, simply the presenting issue. For example:

We are finding it hard to secure core funding

2   Next draw a spine:

3   Then draw on some angled 'ribs'. At the end of each of these describe an aspect of the problem or a related issue. Each of these represents a cause of the ultimate effect:

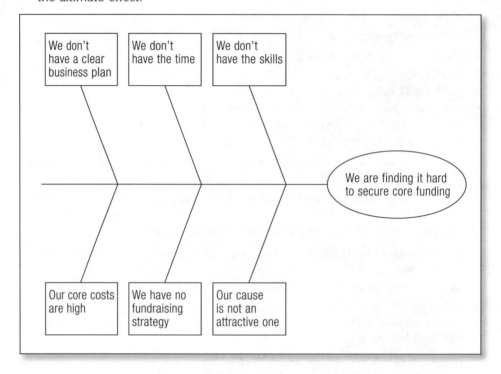

4   If you need to, you can another level of thinking by creating smaller bones to attach to each 'rib'. These smaller bones should represent 'the causes of the causes'. For example, the reason that you have no business plan may be because the trustees refuse to accept that you need one – 'What's the point of planning? We should just be opportunistic'.

5   Finally, consider all of the issues together, look for relationships, causal factors, major and minor issues and so on.

In the example given above, the biggest and most fundamental problem would probably be the lack of a clear business plan. Without that, solving the 'no time' or 'no skills' issues wouldn't help much. Once that is addressed, attacking these subsidiary problems becomes appropriate. Indeed, the business plan could help to solve these issues by looking at roles and responsibilities, training needs and so on.

The fishbone technique has a number of advantages:

➤ You get to see the whole picture, before trying to solve a single piece. It prevents tunnel vision.

➤ It shows clearly the relationship between presenting problems and more fundamental root causes.

➤ It helps prevent group discussion disintegrating into positional argument, blaming of others, denial, misunderstanding, and all of the other bad habits that prevent us from getting to the truth of a situation.

➤ By breaking the problem down into constituent parts and contributing causes, it also shows how quickly progress might be possible.

Exercise 3

Try this technique on the problem you thought of in Exercise 1.

1 Write down the problem

2 Draw the spine

3 Brainstorm the 'rib' issues.

Is your problem now clearer? Has it changed in substance? Has it changed in emphasis?

Using soft thinking to define your problem

People who lean on logic and philosophy and rational exposition end by starving the best part of the mind.

William Butler Yeats

Just as important to confirming your real, or most fundamental, problem is right-brain thinking. Whereas the left brain provides an ability to use a logical and systematic approach, the right hemisphere of the brain gives us access to a different set of talents altogether. These include the ability to be imaginative, intuitive and associative. One way of engaging these 'soft' talents is to use a creative metaphor. This is particularly important in those situations where you have a 'feeling', but can't say why.

We've all had such feelings about a person, a place, a situation. But in a right versus wrong culture, it is easy to dismiss them as irrational or somehow as having less value because there is no hard logic to support them. The creative metaphor is one way of capturing these feelings in a more tangible form, so that the issues can be identified and acted upon.

With my customers, I commonly use one of these techniques – both are variations on a theme. I call these:

> Drawing on the right side;

> Tell a fairy tale.

Drawing on the right side

This technique demands that we try to bring the right side to bear by drawing a *picture* of our problem. We choose to build in a 'creative metaphor' to use the power of metaphor to help us describe and get to the root of our problems.

Case study: One housing organisation in the South East ran an away day in which the management committee was asked to draw wild animals to represent how it wanted to work in the future. One member drew a meerkat because this animal stands on its hind legs to look for threats on the horizon, seeks to nurture its own kind and is able to undertake complex shared tasks as the group works together to make a safe network of tunnels to live in. From this image the committee was able to draw down a specific list of planning, supporting and management objectives to achieve over the next three years.

One of the key advantages of this technique is that it allows difficult or potentially contentious ideas to be expressed 'safely'. It may flag up difficulties that you find hard to talk about.

Case study: At one of my seminars the theme we chose to stimulate a metaphor was 'Monsters from the Id'. We decided create our metaphor around the classic Sci Fi movie *Forbidden Planet*. In the movie, based on Shakespeare's *Tempest*, an intrepid spaceship crew do battle with terrible monsters. Towards the end of the movie we discover that the monsters are created by the subconscious of Dr Morbius, one of the central characters.

Having a little fun with the idea of 'your organisation as a monster' a researcher for an environmental charity sat down and drew a monster with two heads representing the staff and trustees. The heads were looking in opposite directions and while one had a mouth and no ears, the other had ears but only a tiny mouth. This image led to a debate about shared mission and communication issues within the charity.

Visual tools such as this one are effective because they relate to the way we process information. Although we acquire information in a linear fashion – one piece at a time – once we have it, it is processed using holographic thinking. This involves seeing the big picture, making links between the various parts, associating freely. Imagine you visit a town for the first time. Linear thinking is the equivalent of trying to get a sense of what this new environment is like whilst wearing blinkers. You'd get a lot of information, but most of it in a linear stream of 'data packages'. Holographic thinking is more like absorbing the street scene through a more holistic experience. Visual tools such as the fishbone diagram, radiant thinking on page 46, or force field analysis on page 75 all allow us this big-picture, wide-angle-lens effect. When used in a group context, they have the added benefit, of course, of raising the question – 'do you see things in the same way as me?' As the picture develops, it can provide fundamental truths which might not be so visceral or concrete during a more organic discussion. Or in other words, it is easier to misunderstand words than a picture.

Exercise 4

Make a creative metaphor – visit Ogreopolis

1   Take a large sheet of paper – a sheet of flipchart paper is ideal – and a packet of marker pens.

2   Draw a monster which represents your organisation and the issues that it faces.

   ➤   How many limbs, eyes, or heads does your monster have and what do each of these represent?

   ➤   Is it bloated or starved of nourishment?

   ➤   Is the head buried in the ground or lost in the clouds? Is it fierce or indifferent?

   ➤   Does it devour people or nurture them (monsters can be cuddly too!)

   I'm sure you get the idea.

3   Go off and draw the picture

4   When you've finished, it is time to take your trusty lance and kill the monster! Or tame it. Or learn to live with it.

In other words, take your pen and draw down the issues you have identified, decide what outcomes you'd like to achieve in response to these issues, and create a plan of action.

Issue/problem	Situation we want to achieve (usually the opposite of the issue!)	How to achieve it (people to involve, money to spend, actions to take etc.)
_____	_____	_____
_____	_____	_____
_____	_____	_____
_____	_____	_____

1 Create!

Tell a fairy story

You can create a metaphor by painting a picture with words. Fairy tales, for example, spring from the oral tradition of education and socialisation. They have always had a duel role, to entertain of course, but also (through the moral of the story) to teach children how to think and relate to real-life situations.

Exercise 5

Think about a fairy story with which you are familiar. Consider how that fairy story is similar to your situation. Think about the moral of the tale. Does this shed any light on how you might change behaviours, circumstances, plans or situations? Which of the characters could be represented by real people involved in your problem? How is the story resolved and what becomes of the characters? Capture any ideas you have in the space below.

Here is a list of famous fairy stories with plot summaries/assumed moral for those of you who never heard the tales or have simply forgotten them.

Goldilocks and the 3 Bears: Goldilocks breaks into the house owned by three respectable bears (how many bears do you know who wear clothes and take family strolls in the wood?), breaks their furniture and steals their food and then gets into bed with her shoes on. And it's the bears who come out as the villains!

Jack and the Beanstalk: Slow-witted Jack makes himself and his Mum much poorer by giving away the family cow in exchange for five seemingly worthless beans. However, once planted, they give him the opportunity to steal the goose which lays the golden eggs.

Little Red Riding Hood: If only she hadn't strayed from the path …

The Emperor's New Clothes: Let's face it – the big cheese is an idiot! And it takes a child to point this out. Do you have an Emperor in your midst? Or a whistle blower? And what about the tailors?

(NB: This exercise usually works best, and is most fun, when attempted by a group of people, rather than a lone individual).

Reflections/notes

_____

_____

_____

Conclusion

Now that you've had a chance to play with a whole range of hard and soft problem confirmation techniques, what do you now believe the essence of the problem you wrote down on page 8 to be? Take a few moments to write this down.

➤ Has the problem changed completely?

➤ Has it changed in emphasis?

➤ Is it the same only clearer?

To summarise ...

We tend to try to make sense of a situation quickly, sometimes before all of the evidence is in. We sometimes make assumptions about situations, people and issues before we see the whole picture. In order to solve our problems effectively however, we need to see them clearly and within context and to be able to separate presenting symptoms from root causes.

We need therefore to practise 'getting below the surface'.

We can accomplish this using hard thinking techniques, such as the 6 fundamental questions, pyramid thinking or the fishbone diagram. These help us to map systematically complicated issues and differentiate between a cause and its symptom.

We can also use soft thinking techniques such as drawing a picture or telling a story, both of which allow us to use guided imagery and metaphor. This is a good way of involving our gut feelings and experience. Less 'scientific', but just as valuable.

Your FIRST challenge is to get to grips with the real problem, to avoid red herrings and not to be sidetracked.

Step 2

Risk ...

... take some

Why 'risk'?

Tom Peters said, 'test fast, fail fast, adjust fast'. He was referring to the same ideas as Vilifredo Pareto, who in the eighteenth century said 'give me the fruitful error'. These great thinkers, writing two centuries apart, both understood a simple truth – that we cannot progress unless we try things out – and of course we can't try things out unless we are prepared to take risk.

Section overview

In this section we will discover:

➤ how fear of failure stifles creativity

➤ how the ability to have ideas is a habit that can be learned

➤ how success is born of failure.

The person who never made a mistake, never made anything

Only those who will risk going too far can possibly find out how far one can go.

T. S. Eliot

In the final game of their World Cup 2002 qualifying campaign, England's football team needed a result against Greece. Things however, were not going to plan, and with just minutes to go it looked as if they were on their way out of the competition. Then a Greek defender committed a foul some 30 yards from goal and England was awarded a free kick. Up stepped David Beckham and tens of thousands of footie fans across the country held their breath. This was the 'last chance saloon'. If he scored, England qualified for the finals of the competition in Japan and Korea. If he missed, it was game over. Perhaps the football fans among you remember what happened next? A wonderful 30-yard curling shot into the top corner of the goal. What you may not remember however, is that for the preceding 90 minutes, Beckham had had a go at goal almost every time he came within shooting range. He'd tried, and missed a number of free kicks similar to the one which finally went in. But as each attempt failed, he remained undiscouraged. He just kept at it until he finally succeeded. Beckham was able to do this because he understands a simple reality.

He will never score wonderful goals unless he is prepared to put a few balls over the bar, the wrong side of the post, sometimes a few out of the stadium altogether. *To succeed, you have to be prepared to risk failure.* As Anthony Robbins observes in his book *Awaken the Giant Within*, success comes from good judgement. Good judgement comes from experience. Experience comes as a result of poor judgement and failure. So try to get it wrong more often!

This also applies to creativity. The key difference between people who have great ideas and those who don't is not that the first group are 'creative' and the others 'unimaginative'. It is that the first group is prepared to give themselves permission to have lots of ideas, in the sure knowledge that lots of these will be weak. Pablo Picasso may be remembered for masterpieces such as *Guernica*, but he created over 2,000 works, many of them not quite so well regarded or famous. Of course, *everything* Mozart produced was wonderful, but some works, such as his *Requiem*, *The Magic Flute* or *Eine kleine Nachtmusik*, are considered by many to be a bit more wonderful than the rest! Michelangelo said 'If people knew how hard I worked to get my mastery, it wouldn't seem so wonderful at all'. In fact it seems that the sheer volume of creative thought is central to producing the masterpiece, the breakthrough, or the revolutionary practice. Certainly the fecundity of thought (and the ability to produce lots of ideas of all degrees of quality) of those who are remembered for their great ideas is well documented:

➤ Thomas Edison lodged 1,093 patents with the US Patent Office. Every schoolchild knows that he brought us the light bulb. Maybe you've heard he invented recorded sound. But can you name five more of his patents? How about three? The fact is that the US Patent Office still has files and files filled with Edison's ideas which would not work or never caught on – some ridiculous, some impractical, some plain crazy.

➤ Charles Babbage invented the first computer. So far so good. But he also baked himself in the oven to test the effects of extreme heat on a person!

➤ Sir Isaac Newton invented Calculus (at the time a revolutionary form of mathematics), described the precise orbits of the planets and developed the laws of motion and gravity which transformed contemporary physics. But he also spent a significant proportion of his career trying to turn lead into gold and once stuck a needle into the space between his eye and his eye socket to see whether this would damage his eye! (Remarkably, it didn't – although I wouldn't recommend that you repeat the experiment.)

➤ Clive Sinclair came up with an idea for the pocket calculator and the digital wristwatch. Great ideas! But he also invented the C5 (remember that little egg-shaped car?) – an idea which spectacularly failed to grab the public's imagination.

And things are just the same today, in the twenty-first century. The Ig Nobel Prize is an annual international competition for useless science. Previous ideas to win the prize include:

➤ Scientists who concluded that breakfast cereal becomes soggy because it comes into contact with fluid.

➤ The University of Illinois researchers who concluded that 'incompetent people are incompetent at recognising incompetence'.

➤ The Blonsky, a giant rotating machine which uses centrifugal force to facilitate the birth of a child. That is, it might if you could persuade a pregnant woman to strap herself to it!

➤ The mathematician who calculated odds of 710,609,175,188,282,000 to 1 that Mikhail Gorbachev is the Antichrist.

➤ The Australian Patent Office which issued patent number 2001 1000 12 to a man from Victoria, Australia for his invention – 'the wheel'.

➤ The inventor of Airtight underwear with a replaceable charcoal filter to absorb bodily gases and odours.

And (my personal favourite) …

➤ Scientists from the universities of Nijmegan and Bristol who used magnets to levitate a frog and a sumo wrestler. (10)

(Keep at it guys!)

The message is clear. Even the most creative minds that have the best ideas have rotten ideas too! But they only get the good ideas because they are prepared to open up their minds to all possibilities. If you hang around waiting for 'a brilliant idea', but you don't *practise* having ideas, you'll end up waiting a long time. On the other hand if you do get your brain into the habit of having ideas, it will soon enthusiastically join in! As American novelist John Steinbeck said, 'Ideas are like rabbits. Get yourself two and pretty soon you've got a dozen'. Just as David Beckham goes out on the practise field every day and hits shot after shot towards goal, you have to get into the habit of allowing your mind to shoot. Most attempts will sail over the grandstand into the car park outside. But once in a while you'll produce a spectacular thunderbolt which cannons into the back of the net!

So, become an ideas machine. Churn them out. And love the fact that most will be bad. Take risks, and accept that without risk, there is no reward.

Be audacious! … examples of not-for-profit risk takers who hit the jackpot!

Case study: German artist Peter Klasen suggested that Princess Stephanie of Monaco pose nude for photos that were then auctioned off to raise money for her Aids foundation. Most of us would think twice before asking a Royal to strip! But speaking to French magazine *Oh La* Princess Stephanie said that the idea had 'moved' and 'flattered' her. Despite the risk that she may have been offended by his suggestion, Klasen had an idea, and took a risk.

In 2003, The Esmee Fairbairn Charitable Trust became the first grant-making foundation in the UK to set up a loan scheme. In conjunction with Charity Bank, the trust made £3,000,000 available. But what if charities failed to repay the loans? The trustees of Esmee Fairbairn, in true innovative style, are clearly prepared to live with that risk.

In the 1980s a homelessness project called Nightstop was launched in the UK. The basic idea was that volunteers would make their homes available, on a temporary basis, to young homeless people. This gave the young people time to recover their breath, think twice about jumping on a train to London, and perhaps, with additional support, sort out any problems that underlay their homelessness. But what if the young people, many of whom were troubled, having come through the local authority 'looked-after' system, had become violent or had stolen from their hosts? In fact this rarely, if ever, happens (Nightstop is still going strong today), but it must have seemed like a very real risk to the original trustees. Nevertheless, they took a risk and thousands of young people have benefited over the years as a result.

In the summer of 2003 an anonymous person posted a similar idea 'Group Kitchens for the Homeless' on a creativity website in the USA. (11) The anonymous philanthropist reported that he had identified a number of low-paid individuals who were forced to sleep in their cars after losing rented accommodation. He went about 'adopting' a number of car-dwellers, giving them limited access to his home, allowing them to take showers, and using his phone for job seeking. In exchange they performed various chores. Most of the adoptees eventually found permanent places to live. Some got together to share rented accommodation and then made this place available to other car-dwellers. What if one of the adoptees had abused our philanthropist's hospitality or been difficult to get along with? It could have ended in tears, but he took a risk and changed lives.

To summarise ...

The only way to stay completely safe is to remain unborn. Life is risky. Very few people succeed without experience – and the best way to get that experience is to fail a few times.

You simply cannot hope to have a great idea, unless you are prepared to have a few hopeless ones. It is no use waiting around for a great idea to appear. Great thinkers have always tended to focus primarily on volume – statistically it makes sense that the more ideas you have the more chance you will have of having a brilliant one. Creative people practise having ideas and practise the freedom to think without consequences because they understand that this is the only way to achieve a 'light bulb moment'.

Your SECOND challenge is to give yourself, your team and your colleagues the freedom to fail!

CREATE

Step 3

Expand ...

... your options

Why 'expand'?

So far you've taken two steps on your journey. You've identified what your problem is (or problems are) and you've given yourself the freedom to take risks with your thinking. The next stage is simply to use that freedom. The third section of this book offers tools and techniques to expand the number of options available to you. Limited thinking inevitably results in fewer potential solutions. But in addition, critical thinking, if applied too early, can result in 'ideacide' – the murder of an idea before it has had a chance to develop. That's why this section is about using expansive, divergent thinking to come up with as many solutions, options, answers and responses as possible. Only by looking at all of the available avenues can you identify the very best one.

Remember the left versus right-brain model we mentioned earlier? As you will see, some of the methods we will examine in this section use your left brain's ability to be systematic and others tap into the right brain's intuitive properties.

Section overview

In this section you will:

➤ examine nine key approaches to help you generate options

➤ learn how to make sure you always remember great ideas that suddenly 'appear'

➤ learn the value of perseverance from Darwin and Copernicus

➤ learn how to radiate ideas from a central 'core' to produce exponential results

➤ learn how to squeeze, stretch or augment an idea to create new ones.

Think the unthinkable

We must dare to think 'unthinkable' thoughts. We must learn to explore all of the options and possibilities that confront us.

James William Fulbright

Part of our problem may be that we think in 'channels'. We perceive the world in a certain way which may stop us seeing the best way out of a jam. This is what Alex Osborn, the inventor of the brainstorming technique, called 'functional fixation'. More latterly we tend to use the term 'mind set'. Paul Simon neatly summed this up in his song 'The Boxer': 'A man hears what he wants to hear and disregards the rest'.

Using someone else's brain to overcome your mind set

If we can't see an obvious solution we may ask advice from a friend or confidante. But the trouble with our friends is that they are likely to share quite a lot of our opinions and beliefs. Their ability to show us a brand new perspective is limited by the fact that they share our world view. President George W. Bush is more likely to be at home in the company of other free market capitalists than he would be with say, Fidel Castro, but it is Fidel who could offer him a new way of seeing things, a diametrically opposed perspective. It is intriguing to consider, if only Fidel could be George for the day, how might the world's problems be addressed!

There are many examples from history of individuals thinking the unthinkable, of adopting a diametrically opposed view. What kind of world would we live in if the Wright Brothers had *refused* to believe that 'heavier than air machines' could fly? Or if Copernicus had, like his contemporaries, clung on to the Ptolemaic view that the world was at the centre of the universe? Or if Steve Jobs and his colleagues at Apple Computers had believed, as IBM and the other industry leaders believed, that there was a need for only a limited number of mainframe computers in the whole world? If only we could learn to think 'unthinkable' thoughts. The next technique shows you how you can!

This technique involves thinking like someone else, to create a stream of ideas and possible solutions from which we can then select. Think of it as using another person's opinion to help us with our own 'tunnel vision'. The key is to pick another person and act out the role. They should be as far away from you in terms of opinion and outlook as possible. If you are a New Labour supporter and pick Tony Blair you're likely to get the same thinking. You need to choose Tony Benn or V.I. Lenin.

So the less comfortable you feel with your new persona, the better! As Kurt Hanks and Jay Parry tell us in *Wake up Your Creative Genius*, 'your enemies can give you more insight in a minute than your friends can in a lifetime'.

Spend some time getting under the skin of your new character, then ask yourself:

➤ How would they deal with the problem?

➤ How would they understand it, or misunderstand it?

➤ Are any of their suggestions workable?

Get 'them' to argue for the unthinkable. What if …

➤ we become a collective?

➤ ask the Chair to resign?

➤ close down half of our projects?

Case study: How a CVS in the Midlands used this technique to think the unthinkable.

The issue centred on how to get black and ethnic minority groups to attend partnership meetings.

The worker tasked with this perceived a reluctance on the part of groups to engage in the formal structures set up by the local authority, health authority and similar bodies. The characters chosen (at random – see the next technique on page 29) to provide a second brain were:

➤ a plumber

➤ an ant

➤ a three-year-old child

➤ the Pope.

After completing the exercise the worker had a list of previously unconsidered suggestions to try. These included:

➤ to visit the various local faith centres and try to make contact with groups there (suggested by 'the Pope')

➤ to work as a team, share the load, use her colleagues' contacts and goodwill in the target communities (suggested by 'the ant')

➤ consider the time and cost (suggested by – you guessed it – 'the plumber!'). Specifically, to allow more time and revisit the budget to see if literature could be produced in a number of languages

➤ have a party and invite them (suggested by the three-year-old child).

Exercise 6

Try the exercise below.

The person I have chosen to present a diametrically opposed world view to mine is

_____

In the space below now list first their characteristics and then the solutions you think that they might propose:

Characteristics   Solution

_____   _____

_____   _____

_____   _____

_____   _____

_____   _____

Another way to use someone else's brain is, of course, simply to encourage ideas from colleagues (see page 114). Try and create a culture in your workplace where ideas are valued and celebrated. Celebrate failure, because without it, there can be no success.

Exercise 7

Phone a friend

1 Get a group of friends or colleagues together

2 Decide on a problem to be solved. Spend a few minutes to ensure that everyone understands the problem

3 Each person should then pick a number between 1 and 50 (at random). The number corresponds to someone in the list below

4 Spend a few moments getting under the skin of the person you have chosen. Think about their temperament, values, likely mind sets and so on. Discuss these in the group if you feel that you do not know enough about the character

5 Now consider how they would solve the problem. Make notes. Work alone

6 Go around the group sharing your 'unthinkable' thoughts

---

1. George Bush; 2. Ivana Trump; 3. Bugs Bunny; 4. Ozzy Osbourne; 5. The Terminator; 6. Archbishop Desmond Tutu; 7. Ken Livingstone; 8. Homer Simpson; 9. The Dalai Lama; 10. an ant; 11. a plumber; 12. a three-year-old child; 13. Prince Charles; 14. John McEnroe; 15. a used car salesperson; 16. Mr Spock (from Star Trek); 17. King Arthur; 18. your favourite school teacher; 19. your least favourite school teacher; 20. the man from Delmonte; 21. Scooby Doo; 22. Batman; 23. Bob the Builder; 24. The Seven Dwarves; 25. Santa Claus; 26. the Tooth Fairy; 27. Margaret Thatcher; 28. Ghandi; 29. Mikhail Gorbachev; 30. a lion; 31. a tree sloth; 32. Sherlock Holmes; 33. Dr Frankenstein; 34. Lady Macbeth; 35. Winston Churchill; 36. Jesus Christ; 37. The Prophet Muhammad; 38. Bill Gates; 39. The Incredible Hulk; 40. Captain Ahab; 41. Frazier Crane; 42. Princess Diana; 43. a sheepdog; 44. Jamie Oliver; 45. Tony Blair; 46. the person you dislike most; 47. the person you admire most; 48. the person you love most; 49. Neil Armstrong; 50. Alexander the Great

Random triggers

O! many a shaft, at random sent, Finds mark the archer little meant!

Sir Walter Scott

As I said earlier, we are creatures of habit. Once we have learned a way of doing something, or thinking about something, we repeat it until it becomes second nature, even if it is the wrong thing to do! To paraphrase Peter Cook – 'Yes, I have learned from my mistakes, I'm certain I could repeat them exactly'. If you don't believe me consider the case of the 'sock drawer'. If you've had the same sock drawer for a number of months or years, try switching it with say, your T-shirt drawer. You will find that the next few times you automatically reach for a pair of socks, you will continue to open the old drawer. You 'know' intellectually that the socks have been moved, but the physiological architecture of that part of your brain concerned with retrieving socks will continue with its old habits and guide your hand to the old drawer. This will continue until you remodel it by repeating the new procedure. So habit is powerful, and habit, of course, is the antithesis of originality. The random input method is a powerful lateral-thinking technique designed to help us break through our habitual ways of solving problems, which may lead us to make the same mistakes.

Professor Robert Sternberg of Yale University suggests that the ability to make links and associations between apparently unrelated things is essential to creativity. (12) Some of the most creative amongst us may be able to do that at will – but for most of us, it is the chance event, or off-the-cuff remark which helps these links to form. It is said that even the great Sir Isaac Newton conceived of gravity only after witnessing the fortuitous fall of an apple as he strolled though the gardens of the Royal Society. He had been trying to solve the problem of gravity for some time in a rational way. He would start at the beginning of the problem and via a series of logical steps progress his attempts to solve the mathematical puzzle. Of course, because he used the same 'route' for his thinking each time, he repeatedly encountered the same problems and barriers. A chance event allowed him to break the habitual patterns of thought used by his brain and to 'enter his thinking' at a different point. This helped him see things in a new way.

We can't control chance events, but we can artificially engage new chance elements. This is what the random input technique does.

The random inputs can be words or images. Simply open the dictionary (or newspaper) at a random page and choose a word. It is important to use the first word you find. Once you have chosen the word, list its attributes or any associations that spring to mind. Then apply each of the items on your list and see how it applies to your problem. Almost any random word will stimulate new ideas on the subject. Some will be bizarre and some prosaic; some obtuse and some helpful.

The random word technique – an example

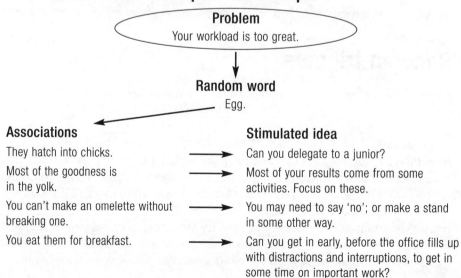

Problem
Your workload is too great.

Random word
Egg.

Associations

They hatch into chicks.

Most of the goodness is in the yolk.

You can't make an omelette without breaking one.

You eat them for breakfast.

Stimulated idea

Can you delegate to a junior?

Most of your results come from some activities. Focus on these.

You may need to say 'no'; or make a stand in some other way.

Can you get in early, before the office fills up with distractions and interruptions, to get in some time on important work?

Exercise 8

Running a random word exercise

Step 1: Pick a number between 1 and 36. If you've already looked at the list below, get someone else to shout a number for you.

Step 2: Find the word in the list which follows that corresponds to your number. Use this word to generate ideas, as shown in the example above.

1. Dog	2. Clock	3. Tree	4. T. Rex
5. Lamp	6. Sweater	7. Gob stopper	8. Octopus
9. Safety pin	10. Potato	11. Tongue	12. Computer
13. Table	14. Pencil	15. Bicycle	16. Taxi
17. Ocean	18. Bell	19. Heart	20. Gold ring
21. Fever	22. Frankenstein	23. Fire	24. Raft
25. Card	26. Doctor	27. Horse	28. Balloon
29. Island	30. Feet	31. Rubber	32. Winter
33. Tailor	34. Harp	35. String	36. Bones

Other ways to generate random words:

1. Go to your bookshelf. Select the third book from the left on the top shelf. Turn to page 28. Scroll down to line 23. Pick the eleventh word on this line. Why 28, 23 and 11? They're the first ones I thought of! Pick the birthdays of three people you love and use these numbers instead if you like!

2. Play a word association game with a colleague. You know, you say 'train' and they say 'station' and you reply 'ticket' and they say 'money' and you say 'wallet' and they say 'picture' and so on and so forth. Play this game for exactly 10 words each and then stop. Count the rounds on your fingers as you go. Make the 20th word your random word.

3. Close your eyes and choose a word with a pin from the following list:

Table, wire, pen, scissors, cup, lake, telephone, Ink, bottle, window, radio, pin, picture hook, elastic band, skirt, wastepaper bin, mint, car, radiator, camera, aeroplane, pipe, football, pebble, skateboard, newspaper, doorknob, risk, bet, shoe, gun, apple, mirror, ice-cream, bus, fishing rod, bed, tree, steak, aqua lung, drill, pill, hammer, alarm, CD, book, flower, song, stone, theatre, rope, flea, motorway, lawyer, kitchen, sword, pizza, prison, vacuum cleaner, false teeth, guitar, snail, refrigerator, monkey, condition, bath, hat, beard, pear, cottage, perfume, tree, knife, toothbrush, cup, bottle, pencil, bed, grass, school, legs, mouse, jungle, sky, lion, explore, cinema, cushion, reporter, curtain, fire, wall, plant, cement, stamp, window, car, packet, crisps, beach, plaster, weeds, smoke, train, magazine, sausage, jewel, puzzle, energy, cream, jug, toy, elevator, swing, lettuce, watch, Clint Eastwood, feet, clouds, teddy bear, wardrobe, star fish, sailing boat, coal fire, handbag, hairbrush, massage, umbrella, ladder, robot, space rocket, iron, jet engine, circus, brain, worm, brick, river, lion, battery, spice, church, kipper, mushroom, swim, towel, selotape, air conditioning, scarf, navel, socks, tank, rubber, gas, strawberry, eyes, hostage, tennis, sleep, spectacles, axe, tunnel, dump truck, tooth, elephant, popcorn, whip, pebble, cat, tram, chocolate, computer, the Moon.

Case study: A music school in the South of England used this technique to generate options to deal with the management of change. The central issue was that the school was being significantly restructured. Roles were changing, new managers coming in, people finding that they were expected to perform in new and, to them, unwelcome ways. Some redundancies had been made. Morale was low. In this environment the school director had to bed in a new management structure and 'take people with him' as the school inexorably changed.

Below are listed just a few of the random words used in the exercise, the associations made and the course of action suggested by each association.

Random word/phrase	Association	Suggested action
Gold bar	1. The Gold Standard	1. Perhaps the director should respect some traditions
	2. It's valuable	2. He should demonstrate to his staff that they are valuable, that their opinions about the future count. Has he been inclusive enough so far?
	3. It's yellow	3. And so is jaundice! Do people feel overly negative and cynical about the process? Perhaps they see it as change for change's sake. Should he make more effort to communicate the benefits?
Desk	4. School desks attract graffiti. People like to rebel	4. Let them. Give people an opportunity to let off steam and clear the air
	5. A desk has drawers	5. He might have to 'put some issues away' and not try to solve every problem at once. Sometimes things put into drawers get forgotten about in time
Stop watch	6. Measures time	6. Give himself deadlines for change.
	7. They are used by athletes to measure progress	7. He needs to agree clear milestones for progress
	8. They need winding up	8. How can he stay motivated? What rewards can he give himself to help deal with the stress?
Cat	9. They move fast	9. He should act quickly
	10. They are curious	10. He should use people's natural curiosity about 'the new director' to engage them in a dialogue
	11. They are friendly	11. He should be caring and 'stroke' his staff
	12. It is sometimes hard to win a cat's trust	12. He will have to work hard

Capture your ideas

Ralph Waldo Emerson wrote:

Look sharply after your thoughts. They come unlooked for, like a new bird seen in your trees, and, if you turn to your usual task, disappear.

Ideas are thoughts and thoughts are fleeting. Unless you make the effort to document your ideas, you'll lose many of them. There's absolutely no way to predict when a great idea is likely to pop into your mind. The only way to reduce the risk of losing it is to be prepared at all times. You can't begin to imagine how many good ideas you have until you document them.

Even the greatest thinkers have used this simple device to ensure that they can remain creative, without having to concentrate on remembering everything:

> ➤ Advertising guru Leo Burnett used to have an ideas drawer. Ideas were jotted down on scraps of paper and thrown in the drawer. When a new campaign was required he would empty out the drawer onto a clear desk and sort through the scraps.

> ➤ Leonardo Da Vinci kept copious, detailed notebooks regarding his observations and thoughts. From these sketches, doodles, and musing sprang designs for flying machines, elevators, canal locks and portable bridges.

> ➤ Thomas Edison had around three and a half thousand notebooks crammed with ideas.

Be prepared at all times to catch ideas

Think about your daily routine. If an idea popped into your head that could transform your work or even your life, could you record it if you were:

> ➤ In bed?

> ➤ In the bathroom – shower, bath, brushing your teeth, etc.?

> ➤ In the kitchen?

> ➤ Commuting – on the car, train, bus, cycling, walking, ferry or aeroplane?

> ➤ At the gym?

> ➤ Out to lunch?

> ➤ In the coffee shop?

Get into the habit of carrying a note pad or dictaphone. Use your journal to record your thoughts, ideas and observations during the day. Write in a creative quotation, affirmation or a technique to use each week. Make the journal your constant companion. Once you have established the habit of carrying idea-catching materials, you will be surprised at what your mind can produce.

Open an idea bank where you can deposit your notes. The idea bank could be a file folder, shoe box or desk drawer. Other material can be added to the bank such as press clippings, cartoons, quotes or helpful hints. You may also want to store your ideas in a computer database. A company in the United States has taken this idea to its logical conclusion by creating a world-wide ideas pool. At www.creativitypool.com you can peruse at your leisure hundreds of ideas that have been donated by people from all over the world, and are all collected in one place. Many of these focus on social and welfare issues, education, governance and other not-for-profit concerns. Of course most are completely bonkers, but some are interesting. For example, at the time of writing, the following ideas are posted on the site:

➤ Community service hours that are part of the national curriculum to teach philanthropy, citizenship, etc.

➤ A standard 30-hour week, but split into two shifts – 5.00am to 11.00am and 1.00pm to 7.00pm. People would work less hours, but shops and offices would be open much longer. Rush-hour traffic would be lessened, employment opportunities created etc.

➤ Family twinning – using the model adopted by cities.

➤ An inflatable flood barrier that uses the oncoming floodwater to inflate.

➤ Jelly-mould instant homes for disaster relief.

➤ The sponsorship of national holidays. The August Bank holiday could be called Airtours Day. Easter could be Cadbury Weekend. Christmas Day could be National Toys 'R' Us Day… (Oh well, I did say that some of the ideas were bonkers!)

Case study: Rosemary de Costa, Manager of Lincoln CAB, placed a sheet of flipchart paper on the staff toilet wall. Staff were encouraged to use the SWOT (Strengths, Weaknesses, Opportunities and Threats) formula to capture ideas and make suggestions. 'The advantages were twofold', says Rosemary. 'The staff knew that ideas were anonymously offered, and so felt safe to take a risk. And I knew that this was the place where they were likely to get a moment's peace to come up with good ideas.'

Exercise 9

My preferred strategy to capture my ideas is:

_____

_____

_____

Persevere

Think left and think right and think low and think high.
Oh, the thinks you can think up if only you try!

Dr Seuss

Curiosity, obsession, and dogged endurance … have brought me my ideas.

Albert Einstein

Some creative breakthroughs appear as a single leap – a 'eureka' moment. In Japanese business culture this is referred to a 'horshin' change – a giant step change in the way things are done, perceived or understood. An example of this would be the business model of IKEA. Before IKEA came along, customers could expect a furniture store to assemble the furniture for them!

Of course, as I argue elsewhere in this book, I believe that when a sudden breakthrough happens, there has been a sort of 'iceberg process' going on for some time before the idea 'emerges'. Your conscious mind, which exists on and above the surface hides a massive, hidden unconscious mental process which works over time to make associations and links to help you solve a problem. When the answer pops into your 'front-of-mind' consciousness, it's already been forming for some time.

There is also a more systematic and perhaps tangible creative process. This is the attainment of a development or breakthrough through the sequential completion of a number of small, conscious steps. The mapping of the humane genome, the discovery of the polio vaccine and the invention of the light bulb are all examples of how many avenues were investigated, techniques tried, wrong answers arrived at and small victories gained before the work was successfully completed.

The Japanese refer to this process as kaizen – which roughly translated means 'continual improvement'. Kaizen is all about small, incremental advances. Strictly implemented, it is a continual five-stage rolling process which looks like this:

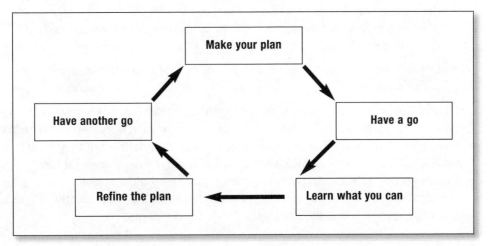

And so on.

Honda call this process 'evolvuation' – evaluation leading to evolution. Darwin told us that the diversity of species is based on the development of characteristics that are especially suited to the prevailing environment and Honda see their products evolving like living things in response to changes in the market.

Exercise 10

Think of your group, team or organisation as a living creature. To prosper, how should it evolve? Break the evolution down into as much detail as possible (even small changes can contribute to success!)

_____

_____

_____

_____

We've already mentioned good old Thomas Edison. He said, 'I am not discouraged, because every wrong attempt discarded is another step forward' and as such was an early advocate of the kaizen process. In other words, he knew the answer was *somewhere* and every time he failed to find it *here* or *there* he got closer to finding it somewhere else. Or as *The Cat In The Hat* said, 'the way to find where something is is to find out where it's not'. So keep at it and don't be discouraged if the answer is not immediately forthcoming.

Sometimes creativity is simply about stamina, single-mindedness and the self-belief to keep plugging away. Sometimes we just have to stick in and keep digging!

➤ Copernicus was a student when he encountered the then revolutionary idea that the Sun, and not the Earth might be at the centre of the solar system. He then spent the rest of his life developing the mathematics behind the idea.

➤ Darwin was 29 years old when the idea of natural selection occurred to him, but proving and testing it in detail took him a further half century.

Edison, Copernicus and Darwin shared a crucial characteristic. They were prepared to persevere, sometimes in the face of significant opposition or repeated failure. We think of them today as intellectual super humans – but they must have felt discouraged and disillusioned on many occasions. They must have experienced self-doubt. And yet they clearly possessed the emotional and intellectual attributes to combat the doubt and keep trying. They clearly believed that their approach was the right one.

This self-belief is crucial to an ability to persevere. A recent study in the USA concluded that there was only one difference between a company's creative people and non-creative people; and that was that the former group *believed* themselves to be creative whist the latter group did not. Because they didn't believe themselves creative, they tended to give up if an idea didn't work straightaway. Or if they encountered criticism, they just stopped offering ideas. This tendency was reversed by a simple programme of self-affirmation, where the non-creative people were encouraged to change their self-image. There followed a blizzard of original ideas and innovative projects from this group.

Examples of strong self-belief resulting in eventual success abound in the not-for-profit sector. You'll never meet a fundraiser who is successful first time every time. In fact one of the key characteristics of a good fundraiser is the ability to be turned down repeatedly by prospects until they strike gold with a positive response. You'll never find a counsellor who expects a client to recover after one session. You'll never find a manager who resigns in self-disgust if he or she can't sort out a difficult staffing problem at the first attempt. In almost everything we do, we adhere to the unwritten law – if at first you don't succeed … etc.' So why should creative thinking be any different?

Exercise 11

Affirm your self-belief by listing your positive attributes and accomplishments. Include skills, talents, and successes that you have had in every area of your life. In particular, focus on the successes that took some perseverance.

_____

_____

_____

Now take that self-affirmation and turn it into a strong belief that you are a creative person. List the many ways in which you are creative. Remember that we're not interested in fantastic ideas (they come very rarely) but simply in circumstances when you confidently let yourself go with ideas. It may be when you invent imaginative games with your children, it may be in the kitchen. It may even be (ahem!) in the bedroom!

_____

_____

_____

Complete this exercise with a statement that affirms how creative and imaginative you are.

_____

_____

Reversal

Reversing the way you look at things is a very powerful way of breaking through barriers to your creative thinking. The technique works on the same principle as Rubin's Vase. Edgar Rubin designed the famous figure shown below, which can be seen either as a vase, or as two faces in profile. Reversal techniques ask you to keep your mind open to other possibilities …

There are three ways in which you can use reversal. These are:

➤ reversing roles;

➤ reversing the problem;

➤ reversing your perspective.

Reverse roles

I once undertook to benchmark management practices for a fairly large local authority. We started with some 'in-the-box' benchmarking – a cross-directorate review to see whether parts of the authority were better at certain things than other parts. One of the issues we looked as was delegation practice, and it became clear that delegation worked much more smoothly in community safety, than it did in social services, although the same 'on paper' procedures were used. After some investigation it turned out that the attitude of the senior officer in each directorate was about the only difference. Whereas the assistant director of social services delegated tasks without thinking much about whether they were within the competency of the person to whom the job was delegated, or how it would impact on the rest of their workload, the community safety officer *reversed roles* and put themselves in the shoes of their junior, before suggesting that they take on a task.

As a consequence of thinking about the other person's perspective, delegation worked much more effectively in the community safety department.

This mind set of 'getting into the other person's shoes' has benefits in many areas. It is said that when Michael Faraday tried to get the then Prime Minister, William Gladstone, to support his new invention, the electric motor, he was met with initial scepticism. In reply to the august politician's sceptical query 'What good is that?' – he said 'Don't worry, one day you'll be able to tax it'. Negotiating with funders is another example. The most successful negotiations come about when the fundraiser has been able to see it from the funder's side – and as a consequence, been able to create the right package, say the right things, and offer the right kind of partnership. Banging on about your needs, and your project, regardless of what the funder wants is, as any fundraiser will tell you, a sure-fire route to project poverty.

Taking on board the views of others also pays dividends when you have to agree on a course of action with colleagues. Think of the people you have worked with over the years. Isn't it true that those who were prepared to accommodate your views were more of a pleasure to work with than those who only saw their own point of view, dug in their heels and refused to see it your way – no matter how hard you tried? And isn't it also true, that when the accommodating colleagues asked you for something, you found it harder to say 'no'? This is natural. We help those we like and feel comfortable with. We repay favours. We work hard to maintain relationships that are positive and strong. So get into the other guy's shoes if you want to win hearts and minds.

Exercise 12

This is an exercise that would benefit from some reflection time. Think of the contexts or situations when you might not be as open to the needs, views, opinions and feelings of others. Are there situations where you have got into the habit of arguing to win? Are there colleagues with whom you find yourself almost instinctively disagreeing? Has this happened so many times that you now actively dislike them?

Consider a recent disagreement. Now try to see it from the other person's point of view. Why did they say the things they did? What is their motivation? What did they want from the exchange? Tell yourself that they must have very good reasons for reacting the way that they did.

Now try to come up with a solution that accommodates their view. Make notes on your musings below.

_____

_____

_____

_____

_____

Reverse the problem

This technique turns the problem inside out to reverse what we are trying to achieve. For example, if we are trying to improve our school's position in a league table, what would we have to do to make it worse? If we want to improve communication between teams, what should we do to worsen it? By making such a list, you may find that you have identified what really goes on, and can see clearly how to stop it, or minimise it.

Case study: A drugs charity from the North West had a number of teams who didn't work together particularly well. Using the reversal technique the coordinator created a list of things you'd have to do to actively prevent teams working well together. The list included:

➤ create unnecessary bureaucracy

➤ don't have meetings

➤ don't take the time to develop a shared mission

➤ don't develop shared procedures

➤ hire only specialists, great at what they do, but unable to understand other approaches or forms of work

➤ foster competition between teams, for example for resources.

All of these applied to the drugs charity. The solution was simple. STOP DOING THEM!

Exercise 13

To use the reversal technique, try this simple four-step exercise.

1. Reverse your goal. If your aim is to 'develop better customer care', change it to 'create worse customer care outcomes'

2. List ways to make the new, reversed goal happen

3. Spot those you do now

4. Stop!

5. Come up with specific measures to improve on the weaknesses you have identified. Make these SMART (**S**pecific, **M**easurable, **A**chievable, **R**elevant and **T**ime based).

Reverse perspective

This technique involves looking at things from an unexpected angle. Roger Von Oech, in *A Whack on the Side of the Head*, tells the story of English doctor Edward Jenner who worked to find a cure for smallpox. He studied case after case of people who had had the disease, but without finding the breakthrough he sought. It was only when he turned his attention to those who had not had smallpox that he discovered that dairy maids were immune. Further study led him to the conclusion that it was the fact that most had had the related disease of cow pox that led to their immunity. From this platform the idea of immunisation sprang. (13)

Exercise 14

In *Pudd'nhead Wilson*, Mark Twain says 'put all your eggs into one basket – AND WATCH THAT BASKET!' By reversing common sense or folk wisdom, it is possible to see alternatives. For example, we could say 'too many cooks spoil the broth'. Or we could say 'lots of cooks will each bring something of their own to the dish'. This reverse wisdom can then be used to help us generate new options. Let's reverse some other pieces of folk wisdom to help us see things in a different light. Consider the following and how they might suggest ideas to help you solve a problem or deal with an issue.

Proverb: You can lead a horse to water, but you cannot make him drink.
Reverse proverb: Not only can you lead him, you can make him drink if you work up his thirst.
What problem might this relate to? What does the reverse proverb suggest you could do?

Proverb: A poor workman blames his tools.
Reverse proverb: Even the best workers will fail if their tools aren't good enough.
What problem might this relate to? What does the reverse proverb suggest you could do?

Proverb: Beggars can't be choosers.
Reverse proverb: Just because you're asking for help, it doesn't mean you should accept second best.
What problem might this relate to? What does the reverse proverb suggest you could do?

Proverb: Business before pleasure.
Reverse proverb: Pleasure before business.
What problem might this relate to? What does the reverse proverb suggest you could do?

Proverb: Let sleeping dogs lie.
Reverse proverb: Don't wait for the dog to wake up when he chooses. Wake him now and deal with what happens.
What problem might this relate to? What does the reverse proverb suggest you could do?

Proverb: Silence is golden.
Reverse proverb: You will benefit most if you make a noise.
What problem might this relate to? What does the reverse proverb suggest you could do?

Suspend judgement

Convictions are more dangerous enemies of truth than lies.

Friedrich Nietzsche

As we mentioned earlier – we are good at making assumptions about what we hear, what we experience and what we see. Once we have made up our minds it becomes very difficult (sometimes at least) for us to change them.

Even the greatest minds are capable of hanging on to convictions against all the evidence. Einstein, for example, was no great fan of quantum physics because the mechanics were incompatible with his general theory of relativity. Charles Darwin sat on his theories about natural selection for many years before sharing them because they contradicted what the Bible said about Creation and the history of the world. Too often we make up our minds about an issue when it would be better to suspend judgement for a little longer. Take the example of the manager who was determined to reprimand a member of his team after working out that 40% of her sick days over the past three years were taken on a Monday or a Friday. He decided that this was irrefutable evidence that she was 'throwing sickies' to prolong her weekend. I had to gently point out to him that Monday and Friday represented 40% of her working week. It was therefore mathematically natural to find that 40% of the time she took off due to illness should fall on these days!

It is possible to apply a kind of litmus test to measure the characteristics which either help or hinder creativity. These include, but are not limited to, the following:

The creativity litmus test

Where do you fit on the scale?

10 9 8 7 6 5 4 3 2 1 0 1 2 3 4 5 6 7 8 9 10

Open minded	v.	Narrow minded
Tolerant	v.	Judgemental
Wait and see	v.	Jump to conclusions

Clearly someone who is open minded to suggestions, tolerant of others' ideas and prepared to withhold forming an opinion until all the evidence is in, is likely to have a greater scope for interesting and original thinking than someone who is narrow in their view, judgemental of others and prone to jumping to conclusions.

The issues we face are not always cut and dried – in fact rarely are they so. Central to developing helpful thinking characteristics is an ability to tolerate ambiguity.

Case study: In the 1960s a man named Joe Pine made a name for himself as a talk show host in the USA. His stock in trade was to be caustic, tough, judgemental and aggressive with his guests. Some put this down to the fact that his leg had been amputated and he was embittered as a result. Others said that he was simply unpleasant by nature. One day rock musician Frank Zappa was guesting on the show. Remember that this was an era when short hair was accepted by 'the establishment' while long hair was seen as a sign of dangerous subversiveness. Pine's opening gambit to Zappa was 'I guess your long hair makes you a girl'. Pine had focused on one aspect of Zappa's appearance and used it as a basis to make assumptions about the man. Zappa's response oozed irony – 'I guess your wooden leg makes you a table'. (14)

Exercise 15

Ask yourself a simple question. Can you tolerate ambiguity? Examples of being able to tolerate ambiguity include:

➤ taking both sides in an argument

➤ seeing the good side of someone you don't much like

➤ recognising the failings of the people we love.

On the other hand, if you find that you are:

➤ quick to defend your position in a dispute

➤ prone to seek closure on issues that are being debated

➤ hold passionate convictions about politics, religion, society or people

... then it is likely that you need to practise withholding judgement.

Retreat to your creativity refuge (see page 84) and reflect on your ability to withhold judgement. Identify at least three occasions when you have succeeded or failed in managing an ambiguous situation in an open-minded way. Score yourself out of 10. If you conclude that your score is relatively low look for opportunities to tolerate ambiguity – for example, you might join in a discussion and try to see both sides before committing an opinion.

Mind mining

Brainstorming versus mind mining

Brainstorming is a technique, developed by an American advertising executive, Alex Osborn, in the 1930s. It is based on what we know of the brain's physiology and operation. Broadly, the right side of the brain's cerebral cortex is good at generating ideas. The left side is better at evaluating. In fact it is excellent at this and will spot the weaknesses in ideas pretty much straight away. Before you know it, the left brain is happily trashing every idea the right brain can throw at it. We have an internal monologue repeating 'that'll never work' and before we know it, we've 'run out of ideas'. In fact, the right brain has just become dispirited and given up! Plato told us that 'necessity was the Mother of Invention'. Well then that makes ideas into infants and your left brain guilty of infanticide many times over, as it has snuffed out new-born idea after new-born idea!

This isn't just an internal thinking process – it is something that happens when groups of people come together to discuss an issue or a problem. Teresa Amabile, Professor of Business Administration at Harvard Business School, has asserted that 'people believe that they will appear smarter … if they are more critical … In many organisations it is professionally rewarding to react critically to new ideas'. (15) Benjamin Disraeli pre-empted this conclusion by some 150 years when he said 'It is easier to be critical than to be correct'.

Brainstorming works because:

➤ It forces the left brain (our own and that of other people) to suspend judgement, to shut up for a while while the right brain does its work. Only when this process is completed do we begin to evaluate.

➤ It suspends the culture of criticism referred to by Amabile, encouraging the acceptance of ideas – at least temporarily.

Osborn spotted how ideas were often killed in meetings before they had a chance to develop. He developed four simple rules to ensure that all ideas were able to survive long enough to ensure proper debate and evaluation. These were:

1   Criticism is ruled out and judgement withheld until later.

2   Wild ideas are welcome.

3   Quantity is more important than quality.

4   Combination of ideas is good; in other words, building on and developing other people's ideas is just as important as coming up with new ones of your own.

This technique often fails because people give up too early – in fact as soon as the ideas 'run out'. I'd like to suggest that we combine it with another technique discussed in this book – that of persevering. As any goldminer will tell you, a promising seam of gold is not necessarily the motherlode. For that you may have to keep digging, even if it appears that the original source is exhausted.

For this reason, I prefer to call this technique 'mind mining'.

Case study: In 1997 a US ad. agency, Riggs, came up with the idea of a Create-A-Thon to provide free marketing help for local charities. In 2002 the event went national with 18 agencies helping their local nonprofit organisations.

The idea is a simple one – create as many ideas as possible in a 24-hour period. A team of around ten to a dozen creative staff whip up a frenzy of possibilities regarding everything from websites and public relations to logos, print and radio. At the end of the 24-hour period, the ideas are presented to the charity clients.

In 2003, across the country, it was estimated that the agencies donated around $2,000,000 worth of ideas to help nonprofits market themselves more effectively.

Exercise 16

Run a mind mining session

Mind mining is designed for groups. Simply choose an issue or problem, get out the flipchart, and begin. Remember to dive in and start to generate copious amounts of ideas. Don't wait for inspiration to strike with a 'good' idea – start with any idea, no matter how silly. If you get stuck, engage in more mind-mining. That is, rather than giving up, or moving on to another problem, simply keep digging, thinking, concentrating. You will find that eventually you break through into another rich seam of ideas. Try the following exercise as a warm-up exercise.

You read in the North Pole Gazette that Mr and Mrs S. Claus are getting divorced. List reasons why this might be so.

_____

_____

_____

_____

_____

Now focus on your problem and get digging!

_____

_____

_____

_____

Structured mind mining – radiant thinking

In *The Power of Creative Intelligence* Tony Buzan outlines the idea of radiant thinking. This idea is similar to mind mining, with one crucial difference – it offers a visual and tangible 'map' to ensure that your ideas are more systematically identified and captured. The fact that the technique helps us actually draw a map of our developing thoughts is vitally important to its effectiveness. In *Thinking Skills and Eye Q*, Caviglioli, Harris and Tindall assert that because of the central role sight has played in our survival and success as a species, we are hard wired to learn visually. 'Show me' rather than 'tell me' works better for most of us … 'when people can see what they are thinking, they immediately become better thinkers' say the authors. (16) And that is what radiant thinking does. It shows us the map of our ideas as they develop, stage by stage. In so doing it gives clarity to the relationships between facts, ideas, issues and so on, and allows us to free associate to look for answers or solutions.

An example of radiant thinking, wherein one starts with a single idea and then adds associated ideas, can be found below. We tried this with a small charity working in London which needed a basis to begin looking for new ways to fundraise.

Step one: Start with a single idea, let's say 'fundraising'. This is the primary concept. Create a figure with the word in the middle:

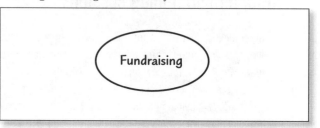

Step two: Radiate five 'spokes' away from the core idea, and write an associated idea along each of these. These each represent a secondary concept. For example:

➤ Business

➤ Statutory

➤ Community

➤ Trusts

➤ Individuals

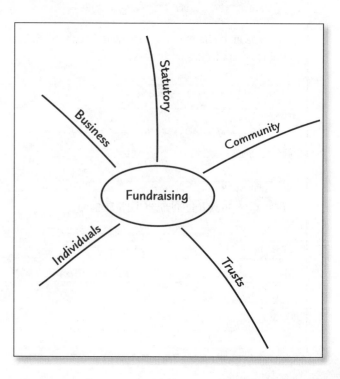

Step three: Next take each of the secondary branches and radiate five sub-spokes from each of these. Place ideas that you associate with the secondary concept along each of these branches. These are the tertiary concepts.

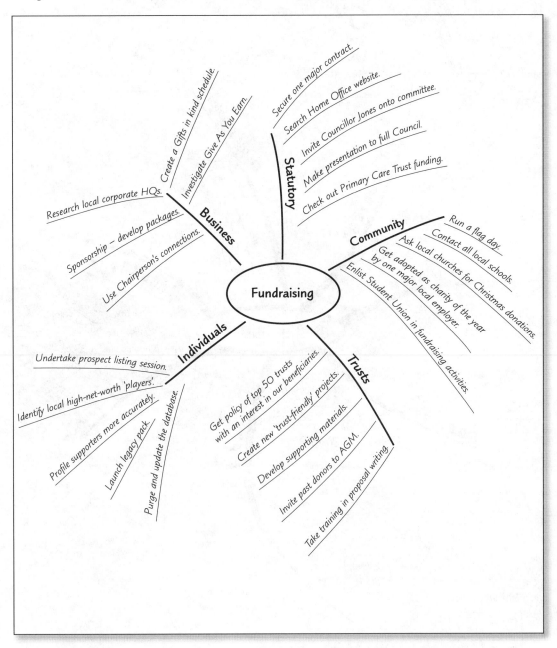

This is a really quick way to exploit your mind's natural ability to build connections and 'map', in quick succession, many ideas. The three-step sequence above took only a few minutes and yet produced 30 tertiary fundraising ideas for further discussion.

Create!

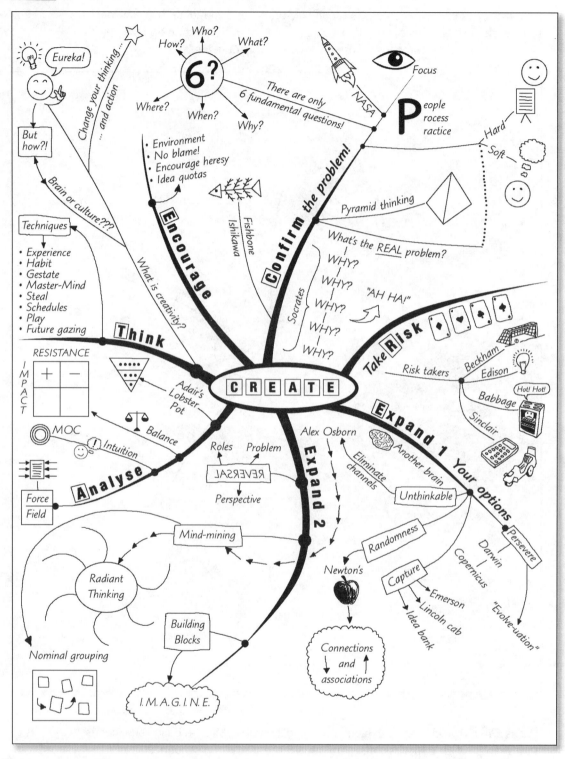

This book was planned with the mind map shown above

Variation on a theme – mind writing

This idea is based on the Crawford Slip Method, first developed by C.C. Crawford at the University of Southern California in 1925. The key difference is that participants are asked to make contributions in writing instead of verbally.

This has a number of advantages:

➤ Because all ideas are captured, there is less chance that the session facilitator or leader can influence the outcome or place an emphasis on just some of the ideas generated. In a conventional brainstorming or mind-mining session it's easy to move on quickly without writing something up on a flipchart, either because you don't fully understand it or you don't really like it. When this happens, it is not often challenged.

➤ People may be less inhibited.

➤ If you keep the contributions anonymous before critically examining them, it takes 'personality' out of the equation. The ideas stand or fall on their own merit.

Here's how I run a mind writing session:

1 **Clarification:** The problem must be clearly stated, or the issues described. This part of the technique works well with the SWOT analysis described on page 61 and the STEP analysis used on page 101.

2 **Generation:** Participants then write down their responses, solutions, suggestions and ideas on slips of paper, about the size of a postcard. Only one idea is allowed per slip. The rules are:

➤ Everything should be written out in full. Don't say 'the problem must be addressed', say 'our failure to communicate must be addressed'; don't say 'we need more resources', say 'we need an extra £50,000; don't say 'they don't have a clear picture', say 'the trustees don't have a clear picture' – and so on.

➤ Avoid jargon and acronyms.

➤ Use short, simple sentences.

➤ Avoid platitudes. Don't say 'we have a committed team' if the reality is thinly disguised loathing!

Participants should generate as many slips as possible within about 30 minutes.

3 **Combination:** The session facilitator should then work, either alone or with participants to:

➤ Sort the slips into a number of broad categories.

➤ Coalesce and combine slips to eliminate repetition and duplication.

➤ Organise the categories so that the ideas in each category cover both broad statement of outcome and the specific milestones needed to arrive at the outcome. For instance 'We should raise more money from rich individuals' and 'Richard Branson is my godfather' should be seen as an outcome and a potential step towards its achievement. They would both be ordered appropriately in a category called 'fundraising'.

One more variation on a theme – nominal group technique

Nominal grouping was first developed by Jiro Kawakita and became known as the KJ method (KJ rather than JK because it is a Japanese custom to use the last name first). It is now most widely known as nominal grouping. It is a form of brainstorming where ideas are first recorded on individual flash cards, or post-it notes, before being shuffled and then grouped together on a wall, whiteboard or flipchart according to what participants think and (crucially) how they *feel* about the relationship between the items, rather than according to any logical preconceptions. Once cards are grouped, the categories are named.

The advantages of this approach over conventional brainstorming methods are:

➤ both left and right-brain thinking are brought to bear on the issue;

➤ it can reveal feelings and perceptions as well as facts;

➤ it encourages participants to think and talk about these, particularly if there are any differences.

Just as with radiant thinking, you end up with a structured and visual representation of:

1 the main issue;

2 sub-themes;

3 individual thoughts and ideas.

The technique is particularly useful if opinions need to be expressed (and have not hitherto been so), if broad agreement is required concerning a complicated issue or if a right-brain 'breakthrough' is needed to get a better result.

Here is one I recently prepared to help plan an in-house presentation skills course for a group of fundraisers:

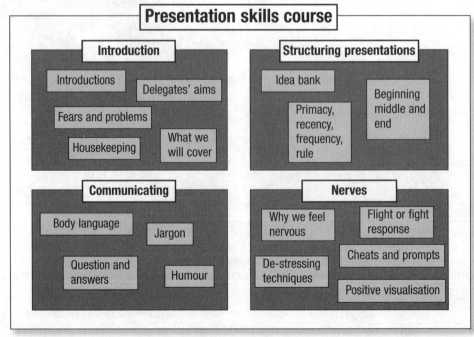

Exercise 17

Run a nominal grouping session

1. Gather a number of colleagues and break them into two groups, 'A' and 'B'.

2. Ask each member of group A to mind mine thoughts, feelings, facts and ideas about the central issue or problem and to capture each of these on a separate flash card.

3. Shuffle the cards.

4. Get group B to organise the cards into themes or categories and paste them on a wall chart.

5. If they get stuck prompt the group by saying 'How do we feel about this?' 'What can we agree on?' or 'Where does this fit?'

6. Get group A to comment on the organisation of the cards – discuss the issues raised.

Think of ideas as building blocks

If I have seen further it is by standing on the shoulders of giants.

Sir Isaac Newton

Few, if any ideas are really original in the sense that they are entirely unlike anything that has gone before. Ideas are in fact building blocks. Even the greatest thinkers take what has gone before and use it as a foundation on which to build the next level of thinking. In this way much creativity is incremental. Take the humble clock for example. It has gone through a number of revisions and modifications over the past millennium or so – from the sundials of the Egyptians, through the mechanical horologium of the fourteenth century, to the first use of the pendulum by Christiaan Huygens in 1657. Moving swiftly to the twentieth century we have seen the birth of the wristwatch, the electric clock and the atomic clock. (Personally I'm waiting for the development of the Dick Tracy wristwatch which will be a sort of cross between a web cam phone/fax and Teasmade. It's only a matter of time.)

That all-pervasive artefact of modern living, the computer, provides a fine example of how lots of small new ideas can lead, cumulatively, to massive differences in the way things are done. Every new operating system is capable of quicker speeds, more functionality and a funkier boot-up noise than the last. No sooner do we get our heads around a current version of a piece of software than it is made obsolete by a newer, enhanced generation with added zing. The computer industry is a great example of how creativity builds on what already exists.

Not-for-profit groups can do it too! Little Red is a fundraising idea dreamed up by Lady Sarah Ferguson, the Duchess of York. It is a character which began life as a sketch on a table napkin, was developed to become first a doll (which was sold to raise money for children's charities in the US) and finally a book. Ideas building on ideas, building on ideas.

> **Case study:** Lion's Club International took the idea of trick or treat at Halloween and married it to door-to-door collections to create 'Sight Night' in which people donate old spectacles to children collectors, which are in turn passed on to communities in the developing world. In 2002 over 27,000 volunteers collected around 200,000 pairs of spectacles.

There are three ways to build on ideas to make new ones:

1 Add a slightly different twist to the original.
2 Add completely different ideas to the original.
3 Add diametrically opposed ideas to the original.

We're going to look at each in turn, in some detail.

Add a slightly different twist to the original

I begin with an idea and then it becomes something else.

Pablo Picasso

The telephone, the aeroplane, the personal computer – these were not conceived out of the blue but were in fact modifications or refinements of ideas first developed by other inventors. So Alexander Graham Bell, the Wright Brothers and Steve Jobs got the credit, but in fact, like Sir Isaac Newton, they had stood on the shoulders of others. It's just that they got to peep over the wall and look us in the eye. The Mitsubishi Corporation of Japan use a brainstorming method whereby participants first write down their ideas, then volunteer to read some out. No one is allowed to evaluate critically any of these ideas. Instead, they must simply build on them, by adding something more. Participants who perhaps didn't have too many original ideas during the writing part of the exercise can make a contribution by bringing their own unique experience to bear and piggybacking on those who did. The original idea gives them a 'leg up'.

> **Case study:** The 'buy-a-brick' technique has long been used in capital fundraising appeals. An animal charity dedicated to the rescue and rehabilitation of injured hedgehogs wanted to raise money among students. They came up with the 'Buy-a-Prick Appeal' – the slightly risqué play on words clearly aimed to engage their target audience.

To help you consider all of the ways it might be possible to squeeze, stretch, augment or develop an idea, I've developed the acronym IMAGINE. It stands for:

Interchange

Minimisation

Antithesis

Growth

Incrementation

New purpose

Exchange

Each of these represents an idea-stimulating tool. Together they make a checklist to trigger a wide range of approaches and the full power of your creativity.

Interchange

Can you slice the idea, cut it up and re-arrange the pieces? Take out one piece and work with that? Can you find a different pattern, sequence or structure? Making parents legally responsible for the persistent truancy of their children was an attempt by the government to change the pattern, to change the problem around and deal with a different aspect. Sir Bob Geldof was interviewed on BBC Radio in 2003 and used the same approach to consider issued faced by Family Mediation Projects everywhere. He suggested that when parents split up, they should:

> ➤ share custody of the children on a 50/50 basis. He suggested that there should be a presumption in law that this should be so;

> ➤ continue to share the parental home, thus affording security and stability to their children. However, to accommodate the reality that the relationship had ended, they should have separate rooms and live in the home at *different times*, each one moving out for a week or two while the other moved in. This would be expensive and difficult for the parents – but it would be better for the children and that was Geldof's point.

He seemed to be suggesting that, with divorce rates running at nearly fifty per cent, a radical new approach was required. His thinking took the problem, cut it up and attacked the specific aspect of the children's welfare, making the other parts of the problem fall in line. Now I'm fully aware that this is just about one of the most complex problems that an individual might have to face in their lifetime – and I have no idea whether Bob's suggestions are practical – in fact I'm sure that there would be significant practical obstacles. But it is the thinking, the rejection of assumptions and the reversal of the elements that I think is interesting.

Minimise

Can you condense, concentrate or shrink the idea? What if it was shorter or slower? Is there a way of stripping it back to fundamentals, getting rid of process, procedure or protocol?

> **Case study:** A housing charity in the Bristol area had expanded to the point where it was offering housing aid casework, an information service, an amenity fund for young homeless people, a 'care and repair' scheme for the elderly and an accommodation project. They had started off as a casework organisation and this is where their real skills and talents lay. The rest of the services got by 'on a wing and a prayer', both in terms of funding and also in terms of hitting high-quality standards. Management resources were stretched to breaking point and as a consequence even their strong services were beginning to suffer. This charity decided to go back to basics, focus on core competencies and concentrate on offering an excellent casework service. The decision to close every other service was painful – but the result was a return to first-class service delivery.

Antithesise

What's the opposite approach? Can you reverse the inputs, outputs or outcomes? Can you change your attitude? Be nice instead of naughty? Naughty instead of nice? Can you hold up a mirror? (See 'Reversal' page 38)

> **Case study:** In September 2003 American illusionist David Blaine was some way into his attempt to survive for 44 days in a clear plastic box suspended over the banks of the Thames.
>
> Homelessness charity the De Paul Trust, mindful of the plight of 'roofless' people sleeping on London's streets, brilliantly held up a mirror to Blaine's stunt to capitalise on the media coverage. They ran a poster campaign at a series of tube stations which showed a cardboard box inscribed with the words 'Living in a box without food? Sounds familiar' together with their logo and strapline.

Grow

Can you add something to the original? Do it on a bigger scale? Multiply the effects? Do it over a longer period of time? Do it more often? Frank Woolworth got the idea for his Five Cent Store when he worked in a provincial store as a clerk. His employer got rid of shop-soiled items and end of lines with a '5 Cent Counter'. Woolworth just took the idea and translated to a national, then international scale. Brian Eno wanted to raise money for War Child, the charity created by Bill Leeson and David Wilson to help the young victims of the recent war in Bosnia but wanted to go further than run-of-the-mill 'mediocre events being put on for good causes'. The result was 'Pagan Fun Wear'. This was a fashion show, art exhibition, auction and 'bacchanalian feast' which took place on Midsummer Night's Eve. Fashion designs were provided by (among many others) Jarvis Cocker, Iggy Pop, Lou Reed, Michael Stipe, Rifat Ozbek and Zandra Rhodes. Music to accompany the catwalk models was provided by young bands and a compilation album was pressed. Only 500 were made, every CD box was hand painted by Eno and had an original Anton Corbijn polaroid inside. Patrick Hughes made 250 small paintings during the evening, all of which were sold. The event was, to quote Eno 'ludicrously ambitious'. But it was wildly successful and raised £60,000 for War Child. (17)

A tool for structured growth

Igor Ansoff was a Russian American engineer, mathematician and strategist who wrote the seminal *Corporate Strategy* in 1965. In it he develops Ansoff's matrix, which sums up the options for growth as a series of simple choices.

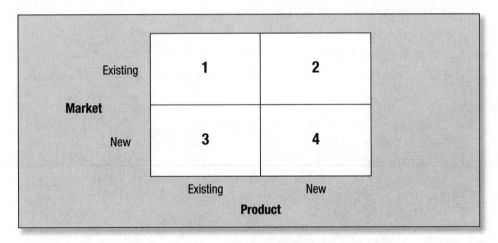

Ansoff's matrix suggests that a business (profit-making or not-for-profit) can either:

Box 1   Find more of its 'usual' customers for its existing product (market share strategy).

Box 2   Find new products to offer current customers (product development strategy).

Box 3   Find new customers for existing products (market creation strategy).

Box 4   Create a new product and sell it to a new group of customers (diversification strategy).

Broadly Ansoff believes that to prosper a business (in any sector) must have a 'common thread' between its offerings. In other words, there has to be at least an element of 'sticking to your knitting' if you are to make a success of something. Option 2, above, builds on an organisation's knowledge and feel for its customers. Option 3 allows it to build on a knowledge of its products. Both of these stand a good chance of success because they stand adjacent to existing skills, competencies, knowledge and experience. Option 4 carries great risk because it asks you to develop a business without really understanding either the product or the market.

Armed with Ansoff's matrix, Letrasett might not have gone into stamp dealing, Coca Cola might have avoided producing moving pictures (it bought Columbia Pictures) and Cummins, the world leader in diesel engines, would have thought twice about getting into ski resort development! Needless to say, none of these ventures set the world on fire.

On the other hand, the list of companies who have built upon their core competencies to develop successfully include Honda, who moved from motorcycles to cars (product development), Gillette who moved from men's razors to razors for women (market creation) and Toyota who simply kept getting stronger and stronger in the world-wide four-wheel-drive market (market share).

So, according to Ansoff's matrix the growth choices for a not-for-profit organisation are to:

1 Find more of its 'usual' users for existing services or activities.

2 Find new services or activities to offer current users.

3 Find new user groups for existing services or activities.

4 Create a new service or activity and sell it to a new group of users.

The same risks exist with option 4 (diversification) as for commercial organisations!

Case study: Over the past 40 years or so Age Concern has steadily developed and this can be charted on Ansoff's matrix. The organisation, 40 years ago, offered what an older person today would call a basic service predicated largely around the delivery of lunch clubs in church halls. Since then it has successfully pursued market penetration, many more older people benefit than did in the mid 1960s when the Council for the Welfare of the Elderly became Age Concern. It has also successfully developed many new product lines, including leisure and learning activities, inter-generational projects, computer classes, financial services and so on. As the demands of the market have changed, so have the things the organisation offers. It has also found new markets for its offerings. For example, individual Age Concerns offer pre-retirement planning for the employees of major corporates. The corporates pay a consultancy fee and Age Concern staff help them help their long-serving employees make the transition to retirement more successfully.

As you can see, Ansoff's matrix also serves to make the point we were making in our discussion on interchanging elements – that it is possible to slice and dice a problem, issue or challenge and attack one aspect of it at a time.

Incrementalise

What is the next obvious step? Are there any small fine tuning changes you can make? Should you try to walk before you can run? A welfare rights project in a poor part of Newcastle-upon-Tyne developed a comprehensive set of quality standards, operating procedures and values. The resultant staff manual finally ran to 70 pages and offered an exemplar of good practice for small community organisations. When asked how they had produced such an opus, given the small staff complement, the coordinator had replied 'slowly'.

> **Case study:** Sometimes ideas grow through a series of linear increments. First we had the charity fun run. Then we had the charity fun run in a silly costume. Then in 2002 Lloyd Scott ran the London Marathon in a hundred-and-twenty-pound deep-sea diving suit. His time of over five hours was the slowest in the event's history – by a splendid distance (no pun intended). The next 'obvious' incremental idea – to run a full marathon, in his suit, but this time at the bottom of Loch Ness of course! And this Lloyd successfully did in 2003.

New purpose

Can you modify or adapt the idea for another purpose? Can you take something designed for one use and apply it in another way – same old idea, but a new context?

> **Case study:** An environmental charity in County Durham took an idea pioneered in America and created the foundations for its straw bale wall buildings out of used car tyres. If protected from sunlight they provide a durable and tough foundation which will last for decades.

Exchange

Simply taking out an element and trying another can produce different results. When Thomas Edison said 'Genius is 1% inspiration and 99% perspiration' he was referring to his attempt to find a suitable material to use as a filament in the light bulb. He tried (and failed) with many different materials before settling on carbon.

So, can you substitute any of the elements in your problem? Try a different person? Try different materials? Different arguments? A different place? Can you substitute empathy for authority – or vice versa?

'3 D' analysis

This technique can be used together with IMAGINE to mind mine options. It involves creating a three-dimensional matrix which serves to force connections between the creative elements of IMAGINE, the 6 fundamental questions (see page 15) – which constitute everything it is possible to ask – and the components of the problem being discussed. So for example, if we were looking for original and interesting ideas concerning the creation of a business plan for our organisation, we would list certain elements of the business plan on one axis, the 6 fundamental questions along a second axis, and the IMAGINE components on a third, like so:

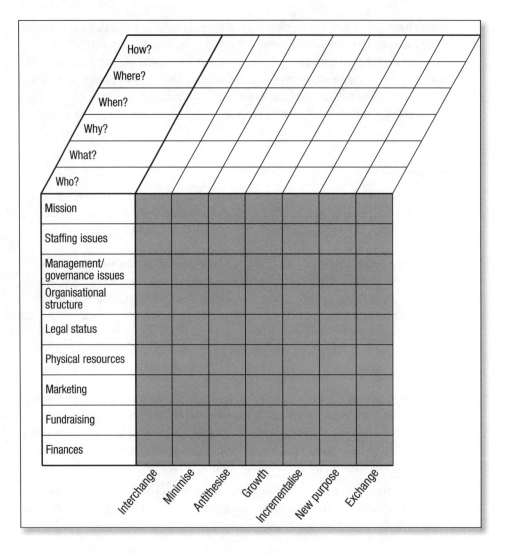

This three-dimensional 'shotgun wedding' forces ideas together and invites you to consider hitherto unthought of possibilities. By multiplying the six questions, by the seven IMAGINE components and (in this example) nine 'content' issues, a total of 378 interesting ways of thinking about the business plan can be initiated.

Add completely different ideas to the original

Creativity is the ability to see relationships where none exist.

Thomas Disch

Taking two entirely different concepts and putting them together to see what happens is often an interesting way to create new ideas. For example:

➤ Bill Mitchell took the ideas of carbonated soft drinks and solid confectionery and put them together to create 'Pop Rocks' – carbonated sweets that 'explode' in the mouth.

➤ In 1905 Dr Samuel Crumbine was thinking about ways to kill house flies when he attended a baseball game. As the batsman swung a 'light bulb' went on in his head and the idea of the fly swatter was born.

➤ Bill Bowerman had the idea that led to the revolutionary cushioned sole of the Nike training shoe as he ate a breakfast waffle.

➤ Bob Geldof took the ideas of third-world aid and a pop single and created Band Aid.

➤ Gregor Mendel took mathematics and biology and created genetics.

➤ Moby took 1990s dance music and samples from old blues to create masterful pop tunes.

In his book *The Act of Creation*, Arthur Koestler gives us as an example of what he calls, 'creative synthesis', the case of Gutenberg's printing press. He describes how the idea of block printing was well developed by the beginning of the fifteenth century. Wooden blocks would be engraved with text and pictures, daubed with dye, and then pressed on to damp paper to create an image. Gutenberg wanted to copy the Bible, but this method would have been arduous and slow (the Bible was over 1,000 pages long). He looked desperately for a faster, more effective method, and his first moment of revelation came when he considered the method of pressing coins from a metal template.

These disparate ideas gave him the synthesised idea for type setting. This new idea, though an improvement on the original way of making an imprint on paper, remained insufficient for his needs. According to his correspondence with Frere Cordelier, he then encountered a wine press during a wine harvest. This new idea was synthesised with his thinking to date, and the further new idea for a printing press was born! A more current example is that of McDonalds Restaurants. Dick and Mac McDonald changed forever the way we eat out by taking the production line concept pioneered by Henry Ford and putting it together with the hamburger stand.

Creative synthesis can be seen in the case of a children's hospice in South East England that wanted to give the children a special treat at Christmas. They took two entirely separate ideas:

➤ that of the Peter Snow 'Swing-O-meter', so beloved of election night TV specials;

➤ the regular Christmas tradition of a visit to Santa's grotto.

The result was a 'Good-O-Meter', which the children were required to mount, like a weighing machine, just before they entered Santa's grotto. If the needle swung to the right the children had been bad; if to the left, they had been good, and were therefore allowed to enter Santa's grotto.

The idea delighted parents (although it was far too serious a matter for the children to treat it as a piece of fun). Needless to say, the meter proved beyond doubt that all of the children had been very good indeed!

Case study: Charities working in the developing world have long made it possible for donors in the West to sponsor particular outcomes – from the education of a named child to the sinking of a clean water well. The Charities Advisory Trust took this idea and married it to the more general concepts of giving at Christmas and shopping on the Internet to come up with the 'Good Gifts Catalogue'. This enables a shopper to purchase an outcome from charities such as Sight Savers, Unicef or the Bluecross and 'give' this as a gift to a third party. So instead of giving your loved one more stuff that they probably don't want and certainly don't need, you can give them the satisfaction of making a difference to the life of someone in need.

The 2004 catalogue included:
➤ A cow for a family in India which would produce a quarter of their annual income. Cost – £185.
➤ A bicycle to enable a midwife in Ethiopia to get around more effectively. Cost – £30.
➤ A children's library in a women's refuge in the UK. Cost – £95.
➤ Six weeks' supply of catnip for a captive lion. Cost – £10.

Add diametrically opposed ideas to the original: the Hegelian dialectic

It is one of the fundamentals of elementary philosophy that if you take an idea (thesis), and place it against its opposite (antithesis), you will be left with an amalgam of the two (synthesis). In this way, all ideas are born. Carly Fiorina, Chairman and Chief Executive Officer of Hewlett-Packard, speaking in 2001, proposed a hypothetical synthesis from two current opposing ideas. Her thesis was that 'developing countries must be held accountable for their debts'. Her antithesis was 'full debt relief … is the only hope that these countries have'. Her resultant synthesis was a 'third way' – that of counting any investment made by a third-world country in infrastructure (such as education or health) as a credit against their debt. (18)

Sparking

The brain is an 'association machine'. It is constantly trying to make sense of the outside world by making new connections, with new information sparking associations with past experience and linking new data with past memories. This is part of the reason that ideas can seemingly appear 'out of the blue'.

We can apply this process to a common management tool, the SWOT analysis, to increase its potency at generating ideas.

Usually a SWOT is attempted using the following process:

➤ A box is drawn on a sheet of paper or, if the SWOT is being attempted by a group, on a flipchart. The box is divided into quadrants, each one of which is labelled with an 'S', a 'W', an 'O' or a 'T'. These stand for **S**trengths, **W**eaknesses, **O**pportunities and **T**hreats.

➤ Working in one quadrant at a time the characteristics of the situation, issue or problem are listed – i.e. if team working is being discussed, all of a team's strengths are listed in the 'S' quadrant, weaknesses, in the 'W' quadrant and so on.

➤ If the SWOT is to be effective, the analysis is used as a basis for taking some sort of action – perhaps to take an opportunity, or eliminate a weakness. (Actually, many of the SWOT sessions I've witnessed don't even go that far – the SWOT ends up in a drawer or attached to the back of a report, with few direct conclusions drawn. But that's another story!)

This process is designed to ensure that all aspects of a problem are considered and that the analysis is comprehensive. This is fine, but if each compartment is viewed in isolation from the rest, then it is possible to:

➤ not see the whole picture, but focus on only a part;

➤ not see the interconnected relationships of the issues or facts recorded in the separate boxes;

➤ focus on the wrong problem – perhaps a symptom, rather than a root cause.

My proposed solution therefore is to add an extra stage to the SWOT process. This is to look for connections and associations between the elements listed in the separate quadrants. I call this process 'sparking', because it is almost as if jump leads are applied to link the four quadrants and what they contain – and a dynamic creative association engine bursts into life.

Case study: A Moslem community association in the North East undertook a SWOT analysis. Long lists of Strengths, Weaknesses, Opportunities and Threats were identified in the separate quadrants. Then 'sparking' took place and connections were looked for. A strength was that they were very highly thought of by the local authority. A weakness was that they had no permanent home. This was linked to a looming threat – that time was running out on the lease they held for a couple of rooms in a shared-use building. An opportunity existed as they were perfectly placed (in terms of funding, reputation and expertise) to run multi-cultural arts and entertainment events.

All of these factors 'sparked' together to produce a clear and achievable goal – which was 'to utilise the support of the community and local authority to find appropriate premises to run an extensive programme of multi-cultural activity. This will also act as a permanent home for our Association'. Which they did!

To summarise …

There are a number of both hard and soft thinking techniques you can use to amplify the number of solutions, ideas and approaches available to you.

Systematic techniques include:

1   Artificially adopting the values and taking on the apparent mind sets of other people or characters. You are trying to get into someone else's shoes and hoping to 'manufacture' an alternative point of view to your own.

2   Mind mining, mind writing and radiant thinking.

Softer, intuitive techniques include:

1   Capturing all your ideas and thoughts as they randomly occur to you.

2   Reversing problems, perspectives or roles.

3   Allowing ideas to spark others.

Somewhere in the middle of the spectrum of thinking, using both hard and soft thinking to a degree, we have techniques such as random triggers and using ideas like building blocks

And remember, if at first you don't succeed …

Your THIRD KEY challenge is to use these techniques to generate as many options as possible. Try not to evaluate or judge them because this will shut down the creative flow. Just produce, produce and then produce some more.

CREATE

Step 4

Analyse ...

... and choose the best way forward

Why 'analyse'?

Generating ideas is essential to the process – but will only get you so far. Ideas remain ideas until they are implemented. Remember that not all ideas are good so you need some quality control. An idea can lead you into all kinds of trouble if it is a bad one. For example, in March 2004 the BBC reported that Endeavour High School in Hull planned to deal with a forthcoming Ofsted inspection by borrowing 15 experienced teachers and and ensuring that 25 of its most challenging pupils were not present during the inspection. The school had been struggling and had sacked its headteacher five weeks previously. The plan made teachers and parents unhappy and brought the school in for serious criticism. Some parents, according to the BBC, called this 'blatant cheating'. The plan was undoubtedly creative, but was it good plan...? (19)

The next stage in the CREATE programme is to use both your intuitive and your critical thinking abilities to choose and use the best ideas from those you have generated to solve your problems.

Section overview

In this section you will learn how to:

➤ Assess 'impact' versus 'resistance' as a basis for choice

➤ Shear and filter options until only the best remains

➤ Use 'critical optimism' and 'judgemental caution' to choose the pick of the bunch

➤ Listen when your experience whispers to you

➤ Understand why 'sleep on it' is truly wise advice.

Filtering and shearing

A simple but powerful selection method is that of shearing away possibilities until left with only one. John Adair calls this the 'Lobster Pot'. (20)

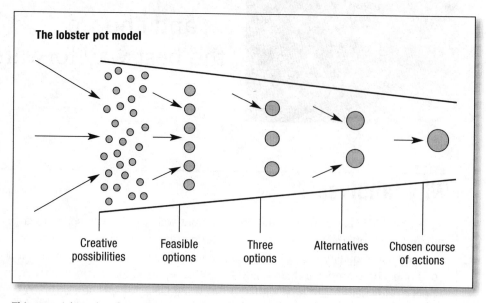

The lobster pot model

| Creative possibilities | Feasible options | Three options | Alternatives | Chosen course of actions |

This material is taken from *Decision Making and Problem Solving* by John Adair (1999), with the permission of the publisher, the Chartered Institute of Personnel and Development, London.

Once again, for this selection method to work, you will need some clear criteria. For example, these could include:

➤ Level of stakeholder support for the idea.

➤ Financial cost.

➤ The resultant long-term improvement to service quality.

➤ Disruption to the service caused by implementation.

➤ The time it would take to implement the idea.

Each of these criteria should be viewed as a filter. The ideas should be driven through these filters, until you are left with only one.

Stage	Criterion	Surviving ideas
1 Creative possibilities	Will stakeholders support it?	13
2 Feasible options	Can we afford it?	7
3 Best three options	Those that would lead to the best long-term improvements	3
4 Alternatives	Those that would lead to least disruption	2
5 Chosen course	The quickest to implement	1

Balanced analysis

*What I dream of is an art of **balance**.*

Henri Matisse

Sometimes when faced with multiple options, any of which could impact in a number of ways on our organisation, we need to lay out all of the options on the table before us. By balancing the pros and cons of all of the options side by side, it is sometimes easier to make the right decision – to see the wood for the trees.

However, sometimes we disagree not on the facts, but on our interpretation of the facts. For example, we could say:

'Age Concern and Help the Aged should merge because they both serve the same constituency. A single organisation would lead to a better use of resources.'

Or we could say:

'Age Concern and Help the Aged should remain independent of one another because they both have fine traditions, separate competencies and separate supporter bases.'

Or we could say;

'Age Concern and Help the Aged should work in partnership to a greater degree.'

I have no idea as to the individual merits of any of the above statements – *it depends how you look at it*. In an objective sense, one of the above options is probably better than the rest, but sorting this out could take years of argument and debate.

With a complicated issue like that above, you could say that lots of debate would be a good thing – and you would be right. But what if our different ways of looking at issues lead us into arguments and disagreements unnecessarily? In 1981 Meredith Belbin outlined a number of key team roles and included 'innovators' and 'evaluators'. Whereas the former are good at coming up with ideas, the latter are better at finding flaws in these ideas. They are both essential to finding the right solutions to issues – but do you think their relationship is always a smooth one? Probably not.

In response to this reality – that the way we look at things can cause disagreement and argument – I'd like to propose a strategy I call 'balanced analysis'. It is a particularly useful technique when the issue is one likely to cause argument or dissension. The basic idea is that everyone in the group shares the same type of thinking at the same time, optimistic, then pessimistic. In this way both sides of the debate are considered, whereas in an argument, both sides of the debate are 'put'. Because the group is focused on the same type of thinking at all times, the usual arguments, disagreements, and positional debates are avoided. The result is more harmony and better quality decisions arrived at more quickly.

Accelerators and brakes

For this technique to work, everyone in the group needs to agree to take on a shared type of thinking which I call 'creatively optimistic'. The group uses this thinking to consider, in a reasonable and logical way, all of the benefits of a proposal – they will work to 'accelerate' the proposal. This is sometimes difficult – people can be naturally cautious, as we have already discussed.

Once the creatively optimistic have exhausted all their creative thinking, it is time to add some balance. At this point everyone in the group throws off the role of optimist, and together become a more sombre set of individuals – the 'cautiously judgemental'. The purpose of this kind of thinking is to find and record reasons why the proposal will have drawbacks, why caution should be exercised. The group now works together to 'put the brakes on'. This kind of thinking is critical, cautious, and concerned with evaluating dangers and risks. That does not mean that it is *overly* pessimistic. Just like the thinking of the creative optimists, it must have a basis in logic.

The rules of the game

1   Everyone must agree to share the same kind of thinking at the same time, no matter what their natural preferences. Interestingly, even those implacably opposed to the proposal must support it wholeheartedly during phase one (the creatively optimistic phase). Of course, even the designers, authors, supporters and proponents of the proposal will work hard and dedicatedly to find reasons why it won't work during phase two.

2   Everyone must work hard at staying 'on message'. It is all too easy for the naturally cautious to find themselves saying 'that won't work because' during the first, creatively optimistic phase. You might like to appoint a referee to observe and spot 'infringements'.

3   Everyone has to contribute to the discussion during both phases. If this were not the case, a natural pessimist could simply opt out of the optimistic phase of discussion – saving all of his relish for the forthcoming critical phase. This would simply mean that the group quickly reverted to the usual, argument-based and positional group discussion.

4   Regarding the sequence of the thinking, it is wise to leave the judgemental thinking until last. If you begin with it is almost sure to kill any attempt to solve the problem in a positive way!

The advantages of the technique

➤ It separates ego from discussion.

➤ It places the focus firmly on working together to solve the problem, rather than winning the argument or being proved right.

➤ It is a powerful team-building and rapport-building tool.

Case study: A charity working with young people in Scotland was considering how best to organise itself. One option was to organise around the things that it did, such as outreach work, drugs work and accommodation. This was the current model. Another option was to organise around the different categories of young person, such as young men, young women, single parents, refugees and people from a black and ethnic minority background. This 'customerised' organisational option was a proposal that had been on the table for some time but the trustees and management were finding it very hard to plump for the best way forward.

A consultant got involved and used the balanced analysis technique to map the relative pros and cons of each course of action which were:

	Advantages	Disadvantages
Option 1 To stay organised on a service-led model	The staff knew how to run the services The funders understood the structure No change meant a quiet life!	There was a lack of 'joined-up' working between the various teams because they focused on their individual specialisms, rather than the specific needs of each young person There was a disproportionately high number of managers in the organisation, each fighting their own team's corner Morale was not high
Option 2 To reorganise on a user-focused model	Better outcomes for young people, as services were remodelled to fit their precise needs More flexibility because generic workers could cover for one another more effectively Higher morale and team spirit. It would be easier for workers to see their contribution as part of a greater whole More focus on real issues, services for young people, less energy spent in-fighting	It would take time for change to bed in, during which time, the quality of the service may go down It may be traumatic. All change is traumatic Some staff would be made redundant

Once the relative pros and cons of each model were laid out on a matrix, it became much easier for the trustees to identify the best course forward. They chose to reorganise.

Exercise 18

Try some balanced analysis

The steps in running a balanced analysis group are:

1 Address the problem in two phases of discussion, first as optimists, then as pessimists. Allot a time limit for each phase of the discussion. As a suggestion, give yourself twice as long for the optimistic discussion as for the pessimistic balancing phase. This is because:

> ➤ It is generally easier (for most people) to exercise critical thinking.

> ➤ We need to practise open mindedness to be truly creative.

2 Undertake both phases of the discussion. Get someone to take notes and act as adjudicator.

3 Conclude by revisiting the discussion. Try, if possible, to get closure and agree an action plan.

Intuitive selection

There is no substitute for experience.

A sentiment uttered by parents everywhere

In 1973, Professor Henry Mintzberg of Montreal University published *The Nature of Managerial Work*. This groundbreaking book challenged the prevailing belief that organisational strategy was a systematic, left-brained, logical cause-and-effect sort of process. Instead, he introduced the idea of 'crafting strategy'. In his view, the most successful leaders of organisations did not spend a long time thinking, planning and reflecting. Instead they took action, based often not on hard facts but on their *intuition*. Film director Frank Capra once said that he believed 'a hunch' was creativity trying to tell you something. I'd like to express the same sentiment using slightly different words. I think that a hunch is your experience whispering to you. Sometimes it is best just to look at the options and then do what feels right.

Everything you've ever experienced and learned is stored in your subconscious memory. Whether you are aware of this or not, you draw on these memories to help you make decisions. You've probably experienced intuitive selection at work if you have been in any of the following situations:

> ➤ You interview someone for a job. On paper they are perfect. They have all of the right credentials, excellent references and they say the right things. But somehow you don't feel that they would be right.

> You decide to move house. You look at half a dozen which meet your carefully worked out criteria (location, size, price etc.). None feels right. Finally you decide to look at a house which doesn't meet any of your logical requirements. You love it.

Case study: In the mid 1980s an organisation operated in the North West offering housing aid to the homeless and others in housing need. Its core business was advocating for people who were likely to be made homeless by the actions or inaction of their landlords – both private and public – in the beneficial area. This sometimes involved suing those landlords in court to get them to treat their tenants appropriately. Funding had been becoming increasingly tight for a number of years, when, in 1985 the charity was invited by the local authority to take on a social housing provider role. The Council offered to give over a street of houses on a 25-year peppercorn lease if the charity committed to raising the money needed for refurbishment and to managing the scheme. The proposal included a suggestion that the charity could use its detailed knowledge of homelessness and its associated causal factors to offer a specialist support role to people who had come through the local authority care system, had drug or alcohol problems or mental health issues. When this proposal was debated by the charity's management committee most of the members were excitedly in favour. On paper the scheme had a lot of advantages. It would ensure an additional revenue stream for years to come. It would tie the local authority in firmly as a strategic stakeholder with an interest in keeping the charity's other projects healthy. It would produce housing solutions for many individuals who were currently being failed by the system. It would produce a lot of positive publicity for the charity and it would build its brand in the local not-for-profit sector. Simply put, the charity would become a much bigger player. It seemed like a pretty good idea. Just as the 'pro' camp were about to carry the day, one trustee, who had looked increasingly discomforted as the chorus of approval had gained momentum, spoke up. 'It just doesn't feel right' he said. 'What do you mean?' replied the Chair. 'Oh I don't know', was the reply. 'It's just that my gut is telling me that this scheme is "not us".'

Predictably, this fairly intangible objection was quickly, if tactfully, dismissed and the charity committed itself to the scheme.

Cut to five years later. This organisation found itself in the unenviable position of having to evict a very disruptive tenant. He was violent, abusive, and probably had mental health problems. Of course he turned to the only agency he knew whose job it was to protect the rights of tenants in dispute with their landlords. Yes, you've got it. The charity found itself being asked to sue itself! When a management consultant was called in later that year to create a strategic plan for the organisation, he discovered that this project had been a constant source of stress and aggravation for the trustees for years. It was a drain on management resources, and despite their best efforts, the trustees were pretty hopeless social landlords. If only the left-brain strategists on the management committee had listened a bit more to the intuition of their colleague who had been made to feel uneasy by this project in the first place!

Exercise 19

Trust your intuition

This exercise is for those of you about to make a choice. This choice might concern your personal or professional lives. It might be a choice that your organisation has to make. If so, it could be about anything – funding, operation, personnel, marketing or governance. Go to your 'virtual sanctuary' (see page 84) and decide how you feel about the options. Listen to your intuition. Act accordingly.

Pay-off analysis

What is the point in climbing a difficult tree to pick apples if the lower branches are filled with fruit? One should always collect the easy to harvest fruit first.

Paul Gilfillan, serial entrepreneur

In his book, the *80/20 Principle*, Richard Koch quotes the famous German General Herman Von Manstein as saying that lazy but intelligent officers are the best candidates for the highest office. On the other hand less intelligent but hard working officers are 'a menace and must be fired at once. They create irrelevant work for everybody'. Manstein had identified that clever lazy people are usually more interested in results than activity for its own sake. If they can find a way to get more out by putting less in, then all well and good. This approach of looking for the maximum amount of pay-off from any activity is variously referred to as:

➤ 'Working smarter not harder.'

➤ 'The Pareto principle', (after an Italian economist who recognised that 20% of a company's customers would generate 80% of the sales).

➤ 'The rule of the vital few and the trivial many' developed by US engineer Joseph Juran in which he declared that some of the processes in a business are super-productive, but the majority (alas) are anything but.

Pay-off equals the return that you get on your investment. Some investments reap a bigger pay-off than others. For example:

➤ At the movies, the top 1.3% box office earners generate more money than all the rest.

➤ You get around 80% of the functionality from a modern computer from around 20% of the operating and system software.

➤ Most fundraisers would agree that around 20% of a charity's donors will provide about 80% of the donations.

This reality that some inputs give far greater outputs than others applies not just to tangible things like donations or customers or computers – but also to ideas. It has been estimated that American companies spend up to $18 billion every year researching and developing new product ideas which will never make a profit. Most profit is generated by relatively few product lines.

So when it comes to choosing which of your ideas will work best, it makes sense to invoke the Pareto principle, and look for the 'vital few' which will give you most pay-off.

How to do it

Balance impact with resistance

How great will be the impact of the idea on the problem you seek to address? Imagine an axis of *impact*. This can be represented as a straight line. All ideas can be placed somewhere on this line. At one end (great impact) an idea might eliminate a problem with one pass. As you travel down the spectrum, the impact will lessen, until only marginal improvements will be the result. Finally, as you continue along the line of the continuum, you will reach a point where no impact on the problem is made at all. The impact of any idea can be measured on a continuum with the equivalent of an intellectual orgasm at one end and a brief shrug of the shoulders at the other. Some ideas will blow you away while others will hardly register.

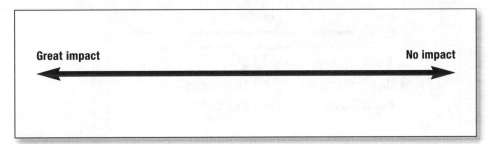

But when it comes to implementing your ideas, it is not just the impact that you need to take into account, but also the relative level of difficulty in making it happen. Once again it is possible to imagine an axis on which any idea can be placed. If implementation will be difficult, place it to the left; if easy, to the right.

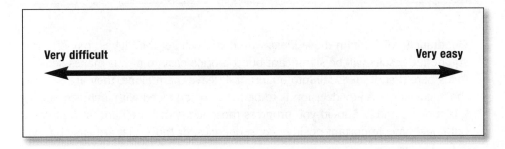

There are lots of reasons why you might find difficulty in successfully implementing your ideas. These include:

➤ High financial cost.

➤ A lot of time needed.

➤ Resistance from colleagues. This can have all kinds of causes – fear of change, laziness, envy, ignorance. (Some causes, such as a strong preference for critical thinking are in fact positive characteristics!)

➤ Organisational lethargy. This can come about because of complex systems, too much bureaucracy, prevailing culture and so on).

If we take both of these elements, the power of the idea and the amount of positive impact it is likely to make, and the relative difficulty in implementing it, it is possible to create a matrix which shows us where the greatest pay-off lies. You can place every idea you will ever create on the matrix shown below, and all will either:

1 have great impact and be easy to implement;

2 have little or no impact and be easy to implement;

3 have great impact but be very difficult to implement;

or

4 have little (or no) impact and be difficult to implement.

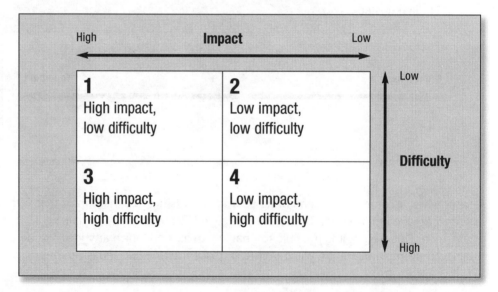

Quadrant 1 will contain those ideas where you will get the highest pay-off, in that square the results will be significant but the price easy to pay. It makes sense to focus here first. If ideas fall into quadrant 4, leave them alone, they are not worth the aggravation. A key decision is to be made when faced with a choice between quadrants 2 and 3. Should you progress those ideas that are hard to implement but could have important positive consequences, or those that are easy but will make relatively little difference? The answer is, 'it depends entirely on your situation'. There are two main factors which will influence your decision here:

1 **Resources at your disposal:** including time, money, brains, attitudes. The more resources you have, the more sense it makes to focus on the big solutions – you can afford it.

2 **The urgency to find a solution:** If the problem is a serious one – say you are facing insolvency within 6 months or morale is so low in your team that people are barely speaking, then there is no point finding a low-impact solution, even if it is easy to do.

Exercise 20

Assess the pay-off your ideas will generate

Below you will see an impact/difficulty matrix. Take a list of ideas generated by one of the 'expansion' techniques described earlier and place them on the matrix. Then decide what action to take.

Step one: state the problem

_____

_____

Step two: take your list of solutions and place then on the matrix

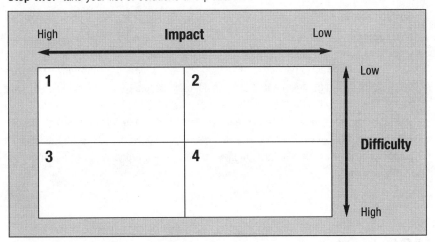

Step three: record what action you intend to take, how and why

_____

_____

_____

_____

Attribute analysis

This is a useful technique when a number of complex pros and cons present themselves when attempting to choose between multiple options. By applying a number of attributes or criteria, applying these to each choice and then scoring each choice in turn against each of the attributes, it is possible to rank the options.

Case study: A charity that published information for artists and arts administrators needed to upgrade its computers. They had secured a significant grant to do this and wanted to get the decision right. But when faced with the multiplicity of issues concerned with spending a lot of money on IT (balancing price, processing power and a host of other issues), the manager usually gave up in confusion and frustration. Her solution was to list the attributes that apply to computer systems and 'score' a number of systems on each attribute, so ...

	System A	System B	System C
Memory capacity	5	7	4
Reliability	5	8	4
Processor speed	5	6	4
After-sales support	2	5	3
Price	6	2	8
Plug and playability	3	6	2
Bundled software	4	1	4
TOTAL SCORE	30	35	29

At first glance system B had looked like the least attractive – it was expensive (the low score denoting a high price) and didn't offer the extravagant array of bundled software that some of its competitors did. However, not only did it have a bigger memory capacity and faster speed (and so would probably last longer before becoming obsolete), it also had the best reliability and after-sales support. This enabled her to see that although the computer system would cost more money up front, she'd probably save time and money in the long run.

MOC circles

Sometimes we don't need to perform complex analysis to rank a number of options, but can do it in a 'whole-brain' manner – in other words, simply consider how we feel, react and think about the options.

A practical way of achieving this is to use the MOC circle method. 'M' stands for **M**ust; 'O' stands for **O**ught; and 'C' stands for **C**ould.

Clearly, to say that something 'must be done' gives it more weight than saying 'it ought to be done' – which in turn is stronger than 'it could be done'. This method invites you to make a series of concentric circles with the highest priority being in the centre, and then place each of your options in the appropriate circle.

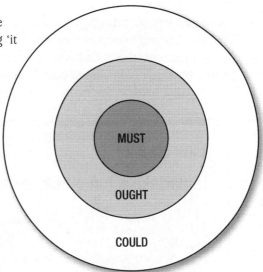

Force field analysis

This tool was developed by Kurt Lewin in 1951. (21) It is now widely used as a critical thinking tool in business planning and project management.

Lewin described how any proposed change in the way an organisation operated could be assisted by driving forces and/or impeded by restraining forces.

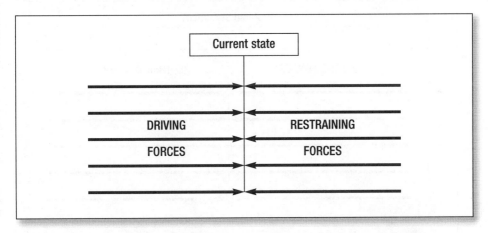

The force field analysis can tell you:

> exactly what is the nature of the restraining forces. Are they to do with cost, narrow mindedness, time, people's egos, power relationships and so on? Once you know this, you can plan how to lessen them;

> exactly what is the nature of the driving forces. Once you know this you can plan to increase them to bring about change;

> whether restraining forces are too strong to tackle comfortably. If so, you may decide to abandon the idea as too difficult.

Create!

Because increasing driving forces can lead to increased resistance, it usually makes sense to try and lower resistance as a first measure. For instance, if you say 'in order to hit our targets and remain viable, we will all have to work harder' this will inevitably result in increased output and lower morale. You'd get a better result if you focused hard on improving morale first – then people work harder naturally.

Exercise 21

Undertake a force field analysis

1   Decide on the problem/issue/need for change

2   Define your target situation – the way you want things to be after the change process is complete. Describe this on a piece of paper and draw a vertical line beneath your statement

3   Identify all of the driving forces that will take you there and list them down the left side of the vertical line

4   Identify all the restraining forces which will prevent, or work against the change and record these on the right of the vertical line

5   Respond to your analysis and decide on the action you need to take.

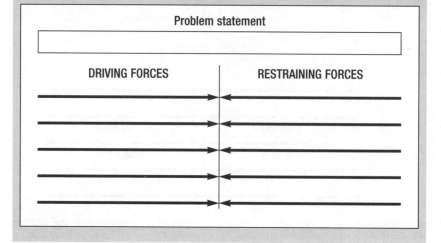

Actions to take:

_____

_____

_____

_____

To summarise …

This section has been about bringing your ability to judge, evaluate and measure into play at the appropriate time. Whereas the previous section was all about producing ideas with scant regard to quality – this is all about choosing wisely, weighing up options and taking the best course of action.

To help you do that you can:

1 Apply a number of criteria to each of your options. These act like filters. The option that comes through all of the filters wins.

2 Balance the pros and cons by becoming (in turn) a creative optimist and then a cautious judge.

3 Measure the pay-off – go where it is greatest.

4 Analyse, and then score the individual attributes of each option.

5 Undertake some force field analysis.

As you would expect in a section entitled 'Analyse', there is an emphasis here on using rational and hard thinking to arrive at the best answer – but there is still a place for intuitively choosing. Sometimes you just know which is the right way forward. Always be prepared to listen to your experience and just do what feels right.

Your FOURTH challenge is to select from the many options previously created and choose, then use, the best one for the circumstances or situation.

CREATE

Step 5

Think ...

... and develop your creative capacity

Why 'think'?

The 't' in Create stands simply for 'think!' This section of the book offers techniques to build your thinking capacity. See this section as a virtual creativity gym with each technique being one of the machines.

Section overview

This section will consider how:

➤ new experiences help us think better

➤ dreaming and resting produce real results

➤ to harness the talents of others to help us

➤ neuro linguistic techniques can enhance creativity

➤ to play like a child to become more creative

➤ to achieve greater creativity through the power of sheer belief.

Seek 'full spectrum' experience

To build and strengthen new connections, the brain needs the challenge of fresh and unusual stimuli.

Professor Robert Winston

When things become routine, we accomplish them without much effort or conscious thought. Tying shoelaces, driving the car, riding a bike, even complex motor tasks like juggling. Have you ever seen anyone who can play a musical instrument 'messing around' – making melodies or chord sequences whilst at the same time carrying on a conversation or watching TV?

The same thing applies to our thinking. The more routine and habit you allow into your day, the more your mind will coast on 'auto pilot' and therefore refuse to challenge perception and assumption. You'll arrive at the same old answers to problems, because your mind will traverse the same old beaten track. Writer George Lois described creativity as the 'defeat of habit by originality'. Creative thinking can be improved by breaking routine ways of thinking, by seeking new and unusual kinds of experience or intellectual input. The empiricist philosopher John Locke suggested in 1690 that the mind was similar to an empty cabinet which is furnished with ideas – all of which come from our experience. (22) If this is so then it follows that the wider our experience the greater will be the scope of the ideas we have, both in terms of number and quality. Composer Sir Arnold Bax is reputed to have said 'Try everything once except folk dancing!' For this reason I'd like to propose the pursuit of 'full-spectrum experience'. For example travelling widely, spending time with creative people (try your children if you have any!) playing games and puzzles or reading unusual material. If you are a *Guardian* reader, try the *Reader's Digest* or the *Fortean Times*. Change routine and disrupt thought patterns whenever you can.

Drive to work a different way – you'll see things you wouldn't normally see. Listen to a different radio station – you'll hear things that you wouldn't normally hear. Read some magazines or books you wouldn't normally read, try a different recipe, watch a TV programme or film you wouldn't normally watch. All of these serve to break up the pattern and provide fresh input. They allow you to experience the world in ways you would normally avoid. They provide for full-spectrum input.

And there is another, perhaps more important reason why you should make strenuous efforts to vary your daily experience. In his book *The Human Mind*, Robert Winston quotes a study which suggests that 'people who had led mentally diverse and stimulating lives were less likely to develop Alzheimer's disease'. (23)

Does your life need more seasoning?

It may be that you live a life on the edge, filled with glamour, excitement and thrills. You already experience the full spectrum of experience – and some. On the other hand you could be sinking into a rut as deep as the Grand Canyon. Torpor may be your daily watchword, boredom your middle name! Take the test below to identify whether you need to actively seek stimulation!

The torpor test

1   Your idea of a racy existence is to order a different flavour home-delivery pizza on a Saturday night.

2   You can't recall hearing yourself laugh out loud since you first saw the bean-eating scene in *Blazing Saddles*.

3   You read your junk mail because it makes you feel wanted.

4   You daydream about what will become of the characters in a medical drama in TV.

5   You spend a lot of time on Friends Reunited trying to locate the spotty youth who first made your heart flutter.

Just one of these could be a symptom of approaching brain death!

Exercise 22

Putting the spice back!

Consider the following

1   What skills or talents did you used to exhibit, which you no longer do?

2   Are there any people who make you laugh who you haven't seen for a long time?

3   When did you last make a new, good friend?

4   When did you last invite someone you quite liked, but you wouldn't call a friend, over for dinner?

5   Of all of your friends, colleagues and acquaintances, who has the most interesting lifestyle and why?

6   What is the wildest thing you could do which would give you pleasure? What is the wildest thing you are likely to do which will give you pleasure?

7   Is there any aspect of your personality or behaviour on which people used to compliment you, which is now no longer the case?

8   What did you enjoy most about being younger?

Thinking about these questions should help you come up with a range of ways in which you can add a little more spice to your life. Trust me – it will help you be more creative. Even if it doesn't – you are a long time dead – so live a little while you can!

Come up with a spice shopping list below.

Within the next 3 months I will:

_____

_____

_____

_____

_____

_____

Do what others don't do

All advance comes from nonconformity. If there had been no troublemakers, no dissenters, we should still be living in caves.

A.J.P. Taylor

If I were Brittania I'd waive the rules.

Burke Shelley

Just as individuals can get into a thinking rut – locked into habits and rigid ways of thinking and acting – so too can organisations. How many times in your career have you heard the words 'we don't do things that way around here'? How many times have you heard that a colleague is working on a 'system' or a 'procedure' or a 'policy' that will ensure that everyone falls in line? Such organisational rules are of course of immense importance. They can spread good practice, ensure consistency of service delivery and indeed concerning some issues, such as child protection or financial accountability, are legally required. But the down side is that they can smother creativity. If everyone does things the same way, then where will the originality of thought come from?

Celebrity flower arranger Jeff Leatham has provided floral bouquets for Gwyneth Paltrow, George Clooney, Diana Krall, Kate Moss and Cher. One of his most interesting approaches has been to turn the flowers *upside down* in the glass vase. The flowers are magnified by the refraction of light through water and the result is apparently very lovely. But where on earth did such an off-the-wall idea come from? A flash of inspiration perhaps? Or maybe just an awkward streak – a determination to be a 'contrarian'? Such a determination can be a very useful asset in the path to creativity. It's possible to identify examples of incredible breakthroughs created by organisations that have thrown the rule book away; who have, in short, done things differently from everyone else in the field.

Like anyone else, Americans tend to look forward to the weekend and the relaxation it brings. Now, however, the last Saturday in October includes Make a Difference Day. This is a scheme promoted by the national *Weekend Magazine*. It seeks to encourage Americans to spend part of a weekend making an active contribution to their community, rather than doing what everyone else is doing – relaxing. People have responded by volunteering to clean the town parks in Monroe, organising food collections for the Connecticut Food Bank, gardening at a centre for older people and painting day-care facilities. Simply visiting an isolated older neighbour or making a one-off charitable donation counts as a contribution to Make a Difference Day.

One way of teaching yourself to think creatively is simply to spot patterns of behaviour – and do the opposite. Fundraising consultant George Smith talks of the development of 'creative formulae rather than creative thinking' in the knowledge-led culture of fundraising. In his book *Asking Properly* he remarks upon the 'ludicrous quest for conventional knowledge'. (24) Here is another way to do what other's don't. Refuse to accept that just because someone says they are an expert, that they know the best way forward. As a trainer and a management consultant I regularly meet people who seem keen to defer to my judgement because I'm wearing a nice suit! You'd think that this would be good for my business – and it is. But such a mind set actually makes it harder for me to work with a client to find truly creative solutions.

Another way of saying 'Do what others don't' is of course 'Don't do what others do'. Why not question custom and practice? The manager of a charity for visually impaired people undertook to arrive at the true cost of the regular weekly staff meeting. She felt that the meetings had become routine and that not much value was delivered by them. It was a large local charity and upwards of 15 people would attend the Monday afternoon meeting. The results of her analysis were interesting to say the least. Fifteen people multiplied by three hours' wages multiplied by 48 meetings per year came to over £20,000. And that was without factoring in heat, light, premises, costs etc. And then there was the opportunity cost. The charity was losing over 2,000 hours of staff time per year to this routine and dull activity. The staff meetings were quickly abandoned.

> **Case study:** In Louisville, Kentucky the local Salvation Army chapter did what others did not. Faced with a number of families who seemed to have adopted 'institutionalised' homelessness into their way of life, the chapter introduced a $5 per night charge for families who stayed in its night shelter for prolonged periods. The idea was that this might serve to 'incentivize' the families into finding work and accommodation. Safeguards where put in place to protect the most vulnerable in the shape of a fee waiver for those who could not pay as well as a policy of offering counselling, advice and other support to help the families become self-sufficient.

Break habits

Insanity: doing the same thing over and over again and expecting different results.

Albert Einstein

As we have said earlier, habit is the enemy of originality. The last technique was designed to help you break organisational habits. But we can also break personal habits to help our mind view issues and problems in different and refreshing ways. Here's an example of how changing a habit as simple as sitting in the same place can work.

> **Case study:** A charity which worked with poor communities throughout the UK had been in growing financial difficulty for some time. For three years they had survived by dipping into the reserves – and now these were gone. The regular meetings of the management group, in which 14 regional managers came together with the head office team to look for ways out of the problem, had become less and less productive as disillusionment had set in. Then a facilitator was called in to break through the negative and defeating atmosphere.

'The result was amazing' said the director of the charity afterwards. 'That was the most positive and upbeat session we've had for months. People not only came up with very interesting and forward-looking ideas for fundraising, but actually enjoyed the day – which would have seemed a miracle just a few weeks ago.' And the magical device used by the facilitator? He had mixed people up and asked them to move away from their usual seats and in doing so had broken the pattern of thinking that had come to prevail at these meetings.

Lay an egg: gestate problems

Creative Thinking cannot be forced. If you are working on a problem and getting nowhere, it is often best to leave it for a while and let your subconscious – your depth mind – take over.

John Adair

The iceberg principle

Benjamin Franklin once said that 'Genius is nothing but a greater aptitude for patience'. There is a good deal of evidence to suggest that the unconscious mind continues to work on problems when the conscious mind is not engaged. A number of great scientific discoveries have 'occurred' to the originator seemingly out of the blue. These moments of truth have then been followed by periods of years where proof or evidence of the theory has to be gathered. The idea has appeared independently of the rigid rules of associative, rational thought as practised by the conscious mind:

> ➤ Einstein was daydreaming about riding photons at the speed of light when the special theory of relativity, in which he described how time might vary, but the speed of light could not, 'appeared' to him.

> ➤ Artists as well as scientists find that the unconscious mind will present a solution, if left alone to get on with it. J.K. Rowling has described how Harry Potter 'appeared' to her as she was stuck for a number of hours on a train from Manchester to London. Out of nowhere, her mind's eye 'saw' a 10-year-old boy walking, in incredible detail, down the central aisle towards her.

Fundamentally, your brain is like an iceberg. The conscious part of your thinking equates to the visible tip of the iceberg, floating above the waterline. But the vast bulk of your mental processes remain hidden and silent much of the time. Then, often unexpectedly, a piece of the hidden ice below breaks off to emerge into the sunlight on the surface. That's an idea whose time has come.

I'd like to suggest four techniques to help this process along. They are:

1 incubate ideas

2 reflect on your ideas

3 daydream

4 sleep on it.

Allow space for incubation

Lewis Wolpert, Professor of Biology as Applied to Medicine at London University, has suggested that because the Ancient Greeks had leisure time (a novel experience then) they were able to develop geometry, the basis for modern scientific thought. (25) It seems that the freedom to think creatively was bound up inexorably with the luxury of having the time to do it.

This also applies to individuals today. The 'eureka moment' is rarely arrived at overnight, particularly if your conscious mind is constantly engaged or overworked. It's important to give your subconscious mind some time to 'incubate' the problem. In *Bleak House* by Charles Dickens, one of the central characters, Mr Jarndyce, has a space to which he retreats called his Growlery. It is sacrosanct and only Mr Jarndyce can enter. The composer Brahms would retreat to a local coffee house and sit for hours alone imbibing cup after cup of the piping hot brew. Honoré de Balzac preferred 'thought to action ... meditation to movement.' Why not create a 'creativity incubator' in a spare room in your house? Clear it of clutter, paint it a calming colour. Take some CDs of waves breaking on a beach, bird song, or calming music. Dim the lights and daydream. So go swimming, meditate, take a walk on the beach, join English Heritage and for only a few pounds a year gain access to the many wonderful oases of peace and calm in the shape of their stately homes, castles and gardens. Get away from the noise of the city. Stop working on the problem and let your subconscious take over for a while. Leonardo Da Vinci exhorted his students to stare at spotted and stained walls looking for connections, shapes, ideas. He considered this an excellent way to '(arouse) the mind from stagnation'. Why not create a refuge in the clouds? Spend half an hour every week or two looking for shapes in the clouds. God knows we've got plenty in this country!

What you must not do if you take yourself off to a refuge, of course, is to stop working on the problem and then fill your consciousness with the candy floss of computer games, TV and magazines. Instead, simply find a quiet place and let your subconscious do the rest.

Pascal said that 'all of Man's problems stem from his inability to sit quietly in a room'. I don't know about that – but I do believe that a great number of solutions would be arrived at if we spent a bit more time in quiet meditation. As Professor Robert Winston has remarked, the tiny electrical impulse of an original thought is often lost in the maelstrom of conscious left-brain chatter – and when this happens the 'Aha-ha! moment' is completely drowned out.

Exercise 23

Create a refuge from the sound and fury where you can go to think creatively

Location: this might be a room, a place (the woods, the beach, the park), or an activity, such as a long hot bath or a trip to the gym.

Environmental preparation: do you need to dim the lights, play music, surround yourself with certain perfumes, or paint a room a specific colour?

People: you may want to be alone to think. Or it may be that there are people who stimulate your creative juices. Can you find ways to spend more time with them, to talk, discuss, bounce ideas around?

Describe your refuge in as much detail as you can below. What actions do you have to take?

_____

_____

_____

_____

Try a little quiet reflection

Exercise 24

Think of an experience when you plumped for the wrong option. You may have given up looking for a solution too early, or taken action without considering all the consequences. Think of arguments that you've had, decisions that you have made, relationships you've begun or ended, commitments you've entered into – which, with hindsight, you think could, and should have turned out better. Analyse your issues and your response at the time in the space below. Then think about how you might have acted if you had taken more time or reflected some more!

Issue/experience	How I acted/behaved	How could I have behaved?
_____	_____	_____
_____	_____	_____
_____	_____	_____

Why is reflection time so important?

David Kolb's model of the learning cycle has become a standard point of reference regarding how we come to understand our experiences, and modify the way we act as a consequence. It applies to individuals, teams and organisations. (26)

Kolb's learning cycle suggests four phases in this process.

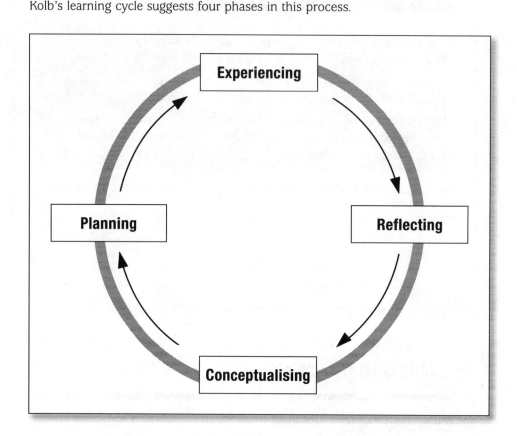

Stage 1: experiencing

This is concerned only with the completion of the task. During this stage we tend to concentrate on taking action rather than thinking about it.

Stage 2: reflecting

In this stage we review what has been done and reflect on the experience. We ask ourselves, what went on, what did we notice?

Stage 3: conceptualising

This stage is about interpreting the experience. We decide what it means. We gain an understanding. At this stage we say 'the problem with our approach is …'

Stage 4: planning

This stage enables us to take our modified understanding and make predictions about 'the next time'. At this stage we say 'we should try it this way' next time.

Getting the balance right

If you spend too long in any of the parts of the cycle your learning will get stuck. For example, if you spend too long thinking about 'what went on' you might not arrive at 'how we should do it next time'.

At the same time, if you miss out any of the elements, then the learning will become dislocated and you will find yourselves repeating mistakes instead of learning from them.

This is what happens if one is under too much pressure, there isn't enough time in the day or one is continually and inappropriately interrupted. We miss out on the reflection time – and mistakes keep on happening.

Daydream

Einstein used to undertake what he called 'thought experiments'. From within a dusty office in the Swiss Patent Office, and without the benefit of any scientific equipment or books, he tested his theories on relativity, space and time.

> **Case study:** Whilst with the Royal National Institute for the Blind, Gareth Edwards encouraged colleagues to wander in the countryside with a notebook and pencil, for one day per month. Gareth told me that the biggest problem he encountered from his staff was guilt. 'But the outcomes we achieved were incredible. People would come back and fill flipchart after flipchart with ideas to improve our fundraising practice and process.'

Sleep on it

> *Sleep is the best meditation.*
>
> Dalai Lama

On one level this is simply related to what we said earlier about withholding judgement. Sometimes we make our mind up far too quickly, jump in without giving full thought to the consequences and then suffer those consequences! So the solution is simple. Look at a problem, decide on the answer – then do nothing – at least until you've had time to think it over.

That's one very good reason to defer a decision overnight. However, there is another. When we sleep we dream and some researchers suggest that dreaming is important to the reinforcement of learning and understanding. (27) And perhaps even more to the point, if you scrimp on sleep and burn the candle at both ends then you are very unlikely to be at your best the next day. It is not for nothing that poets have, over the ages, variously referred to sleep as 'the watering place of the soul', 'nature's soft nurse' and 'the certain knot of peace, the baiting-place of wits'.

The power of dreams

Dreams do not follow the ordinary rules of rational thought but rather allow the unconscious mind to come into its own. In his seminal work on creativity, *The Act of Creation*, Arthur Koestler tells us of the case of Friedrich August von Kekule, who had for years tried to crack the problem of identifying the atomic structure of benzene. One day, while dozing by the fire, Kekule had a dream…

> I turned my chair to the fire [after having worked on the problem for some time] and dozed. Again the atoms were gambolling before my eyes. This time the smaller groups kept modestly to the background. My mental eye, rendered more acute by repeated vision of this kind, could not distinguish larger structures, of manifold conformation; long rows, sometimes more closely fitted together; all twining and twisting in snakelike motion. But look! What was that? One of the snakes had seized hold of its own tail, and the form whirled mockingly before my eyes. As if by a flash of lightning I awoke. Let us learn to dream, gentlemen.

The snakes represented the answer (benzene is formed from a 'ring' of carbon atoms). The theory appears to suggest that Kekule already knew the answer but couldn't 'see the wood for the trees'. In the half world of sleep a number of things were allowed to happen. His subconscious (which notices and stores everything!) found a voice; his chattering left brain was subdued and docile; his experience whispered its soft wisdom – and all these factors served to break off a piece of the iceberg from below the waterline and let it float into the light.

Develop your powers of perception

Most of the mistakes in thinking are inadequacies of perception rather than mistakes of logic.

Edward de Bono

Our brain is constantly processing data and trying to make sense of it. Any data, be it visual, auditory or otherwise, that comes our way, is slotted into our conceptual model of the world. The problem is that there is so much data, our brains sometimes take a short cut and make assumptions. To a degree, we go through life making judgements based on first impressions, but we could understand problems and possible solutions so much better if we took the time to perceive accurately what was going on.

Exercise 25

A little warm up

Notice as many things around you that begin with the letter 'P'. You have 60 seconds.

Exercise 26

Developing perception

Pick up an object from your desk – a calculator, pen, CD ROM box – it doesn't matter. Look at it for five seconds. Now take a pen and paper, put the item out of sight, and write a description of the item.

_____

_____

_____

_____

_____

Now put the paper to one side and pick up the item again. This time really look at it. Consider its shape, colour, weight, size, texture, structure, construction and physical condition. Study it for three minutes. Now put it to one side, forget about it, and go about your business. In one hour's time write a description of the object in the space below – but without looking at the object again. Take your time to remember the detail. Write your description in as much detail as possible.

_____

_____

_____

_____

_____

Aren't you amazed at the degree of detail you were able to conjure up? That's because you had invested just a little time, one hour ago, trying to see the real qualities of the object, rather than simply and quickly categorising it as 'pen' 'calculator' or whatever.

Get used to thinking more deeply about issues. Better still, get into the habit of thinking more deeply about the people involved in the issues.

Why rely on just your own brain?
Create a mastermind alliance

Clear thinking so often emerges from collectives of great minds.

Carly Fiorina, Chairman and CEO, Hewlett-Packard

Lean on me.

Sam Cooke

American author Napoleon Hill, author of *Think and Grow Rich*, acted as an advisor to many US presidents and captains of industry, and as a writer, speaker and businessman created a fortune for himself in the first half of the twentieth century. He went on record as describing one of his key secrets of success. He talked about the 'mastermind principle' – the creation of a pool of knowledge, experience and skill, in the shape of a group of other people, on which to draw to solve problems and find success. 'Nobody rises above mediocrity, who does not learn to use the brains of other people', said Napoleon. Perhaps another way of putting this is 'if two people in the same team are thinking alike – then one of them isn't necessary'.

The following all used the mastermind principle to solve problems:

➤ Andrew Carnegie – in his day, the world's richest man, Carnegie created what he called his 'mastermind group' – a collection of 20 experts, each one of whom brought a different skill set to the business of making and selling steel.

➤ Any British prime minister you care to name – the cabinet system brings (in theory at least) the brightest brains in a political party together to pool opinions, thoughts and knowledge. Clement Atlee described the job of the prime minister simply as drawing these together and seeking consensus.

➤ Gilbert and Sullivan, Bernstein and Sondheim, Lennon and McCartney and John and Taupin – all these are great songwriting teams who brought complementary skills to the creative process and (usually at least) performed better as parts of a larger creative 'mind' than when they were left to draw on their own resources.

The advantages of a mastermind alliance

➤ **Synergy.** An effective mastermind alliance is greater than the sum of its parts. You've experienced this whenever you've sat with someone else and something they have said has sparked an idea in your head – or vice versa. That's the mastermind at work.

➤ **A wider intellectual gene pool.** Quite simply, more heads equal more experience, more varied expertise and a wider range of skill.

The rules for a mastermind alliance

There are some rules to get the most from a virtual mastermind:

1 The best masterminds share a common purpose or goal. The relationship is active, not passive.

2 No one owns the mastermind. It is jointly and severally owned. The thinking is reciprocal – and everyone in the alliance feels free to draw upon the advice and expertise of the others when they need it.

3 A certain amount of creative tension is not a bad thing in a mastermind group. For a start, you really don't want everyone thinking the same. The best group will be reasonably challenging with a mixture of intuitive and analytical thinking preferences, right and left-brain, conceptual and experiential thinking styles. One problem that managers who dislike conflict bring upon themselves is that they tend to surround themselves with people who think like themselves; great for an easy life – not necessarily so good if you have difficult challenges to address. Dorothy Leonard and Susan Straus, two US management thinkers, call this the 'comfortable clone syndrome'. Instead they promote what they call 'whole brained teams', (28) teams filled with people who think and approach problems differently, which is really just another way of describing what Napoleon Hill was talking about 70 years ago.

Managing a mastermind group

Once again there are some simple principles, which if applied, can make a truly diverse mastermind group work better. For example:

1 Constantly re-affirm the common goal.

2 Never get sucked into process for its own sake. If you have a meeting, make sure that there is a real reason for the meeting. (Too many team meetings happen because ... well because they do, that's all).

3 Have explicit rules for managing discussion and argument. For example:

> all opinions are legitimate;

> all disagreements are legitimate;

> there are no taboo subjects;

> all assumptions can be questioned;

> there is no blame, only learning;

> OK we have the right answer. Now let's find the SECOND right answer.

4 Allow enough time for both divergent thinking (option generation) and convergent thinking (choosing the best option).

Case study: The Wishing Well Appeal raised £54 million for the Great Ormond Street children's hospital in London. To achieve this took much more than a talented Appeal Director (Marion Allford) a dedicated, energetic and well-connected Appeal Chairman (Jim Prior) and a strong fundraising team (12 in total), all of which were in evidence. It also took the application of the mastermind principle, as key people were recruited from the City, trusts, commerce and industry to head up the various appeal panels. In addition a core group which included Allford, Prior and Sir Anthony Tippet (General Manager of the hospital) drove the strategic thinking. Allford said of the process 'I believe that the best answers to any problem come from a collection of minds, correctly focused, rather than from one individual'. (29)

Exercise 27

Who could you consider for membership of your virtual 'mastermind' brain? List a collection of candidate experts, wise heads, specialists and friends to whom you could turn for advice, support and help. Think about contacts that you have in the following areas:

➤ Local government   ➤ Business

➤ Education   ➤ Media

➤ Church   ➤ Charitable trusts

_____

_____

_____

_____

_____

Anchor your creativity

Neuro linguistic programming (NLP) is a set of techniques designed to maximise what the originators sum up as 'human excellence'. It is a way of identifying helpful and unhelpful patterns within our language, thoughts and behaviour. Once we understand what drives us to think and act in certain ways, we can learn to take action to improve the outcomes we want and achieve the results we want. One technique within NLP that is useful in helping to stimulate creative thinking is that of 'anchoring'.

NLP suggests that we can find 'anchors' to a particular state of mind and, by summoning the anchor, return to that state of mind. For example, Haydn would always dress in his best formal clothes before attempting to compose. Once he associated these clothes with the act of composition, then the music was 'triggered'.

The process is a bit like that used by psychologist I.P. Pavlov, who experimented by ringing a bell every time he fed a group of dogs. This continued for many days, until, at a later stage, he began to ring the bell without providing food at the same time. He found that the dogs would salivate just as if food were present. The association of the bell and food was so strong that a physiological response was triggered. An 'anchor' can do the same for you by triggering your creativity by recalling the conditions that help you to be more creative.

Exercise 28

Find your creative anchor

The next time you find yourself being creative, e.g. when you notice it's easy to generate a lot of ideas or you're finding it easy to elaborate on an idea, take a note of:

➤ your body posture

➤ the context

➤ your physical environment

➤ the people you are with

➤ the time of day.

Record the sights, sounds and smells that surround you. Try to recreate this environment the next time you need to be creative.

Exercise 29

US President Harry Truman said once that he had a 'foxhole in his mind'. This was a virtual sanctuary – an inner place were he could shelter from the problems and storms of the presidential office. To find your own inner sanctuary you need to follow the following steps:

1 Relax

2 Breath deeply. Close your eyes

3 Visualise yourself in the ideal environment for maximum creativity.

This place may be a real memory or an imagined place. It may be a favourite beach, forest glade or mountain top. It may be an invented room filled with your favourite objects. Go into as much detail as you can. Imagine the sensations you'd feel in this place. What does it smell like? What is the temperature like? If outside, does the wind blow in your face? What sounds can you hear? If indoors, describe the furniture, what pictures are on the walls? Is there a fire in the grate? And so on and so forth. Make this place as personal and vivid as you can. Now in future when you need a virtual escape to a place that will stimulate your creativity – you just have to shut your eyes and you are there!

Describe your virtual sanctuary

_____

_____

_____

_____

_____

Case study: Older Active People, based in Leeds, goes one stage further than merely imagining an environment conducive to creativity. Once a year the whole team goes walking in the hills to throw around ideas, discuss issues, and toy with problems. Fiona Serao, one of the management team, told me that getting out of the office environment had a number of benefits, including:

➤ The line between 'management' and 'frontline' roles was blurred. People felt more able to speak and to listen

➤ There were no interruptions from telephones, clients etc.

➤ Any patterns of responding negatively to ideas were broken, because the usual anchors for such behaviour (associated with being in the office environment) were not in place.

'Some of us thought that it would be a waste of time until we tried it', says Fiona. 'Now, not only is the annual hill walk considered a treat – but also great work gets done. Not only that but we get a pint in a country pub at the end!'

Keep inspirational company

*Our chief want is someone who will **inspire** us to be what we know we could be.*

Ralph Waldo Emerson

You've probably heard the expression that a pessimist and an optimist when faced with half a cup of water will see two different things. The pessimist sees a glass which is half empty, but the optimist sees a glass which is half full.

The same kind of attitudinal dichotomy can be seen among those who allow themselves to be creative and those who do not. Faced with an interesting but unproved idea there are those of us who will instinctively say 'let's try it' – and there are those who will say 'that will never work'.

Your ability to be creative will to some degree depend on the quality of the thinking that surrounds you. If you are surrounded by critical 'nay sayers', it will be very difficult to remain positive and creative. If however, on the other hand, you hang out with people who see glasses that are half full when it comes to new ideas, then your chances of successfully nurturing your creativity increase many fold.

The challenge is of course, as we discussed earlier in this book, that it is easier to think critically. The world is full of people who are trained to play it safe, run with the crowd and think in familiar and comfortable patterns. But let me encourage you! There are many people among us who *do* think differently. You don't even have to find them. If you begin to follow some of the guidelines developed in these pages, they will come to you. Think about it. Over the years, you've gravitated towards people who tend to like the same pastimes as you do, have similar backgrounds or experiences to you, have broadly the same political, religious or social values as you do. You have, without consciously thinking about it, identified these people from among everyone you've met, singled them out and struck up a relationship. You have found that they are like you and that you like them, so you've hung out together. The same applies to people who think positively about creativity. Start to notice that 'let's give it a try' mentality among your colleagues, friends and people that you meet. Share ideas with those individuals whom you find thinking this way. Try to spend more time with them. Involve them in your plans and projects. Not only will you find that they inspire you, you'll probably find that you end up inspiring them!

Exercise 30

Keep inspirational company

In the left-hand column below list below the people you currently know who you think have an open mind, welcome new ideas or approaches, or are able to think 'out of the box'. In the right-hand column, list people you know who are negative about new ideas, don't like risk, start sentences with 'But …' or generally bring a lack of enthusiasm to things that may disrupt their normal work or social patterns.

_____   _____

_____   _____

_____   _____

_____   _____

Now, make plans to spend a little less time with those on the right, and a little more time with those on the left!

What if you don't know any inspirational people?

Well it is possible I suppose (but not very likely).

Nietzsche said that we go through life in a constant state of becoming. We never exhaust our potential – and we are always capable of surprising ourselves – and others. When I was at university we had a 76-year-old fresher. Mrs Hargreaves (for such was her name) had spent her life as a cleaner, always loved books, and upon retiring, had decided finally to get the education she'd missed first time around. She _became_ inspirational. Ghandi was a provincial lawyer before taking on the British state and winning independence for India. He too, but on a far greater scale, became inspirational at a fairly advanced stage in his life.

If you look hard enough, even the most ordinary person will offer an insight, or a thought, or share an experience, which you can use to inspire you. Sometimes the most inspirational people are the most ordinary. Here's a suggestion. Show your list of potential solutions to someone who is not an expert in your field. Experts think deeply – and sometimes narrowly. Someone ignorant of what they are supposed to think is free to ask the simplest questions and to question assumptions. Assumptions are, as we know, dangerous. As Mark Twain said 'It aint what we don't know that hurts us. It's what we know for sure _that aint so_'.

Stand and deliver.
Why you should steal the best ideas of others!

I have stolen Ideas from every book I have ever read. My principle ... is 'Read like a butterfly, write like a bee', and if (my) story contains any honey, it is entirely because of the quality of the nectar I have found.

Award-winning author Philip Pullman

Let's face it – it is not very often that a truly original thought comes along. There are six billion living people on the planet and there have been around a hundred generations of dead ones since recorded history began, so it would be pretty cool (although unlikely) if you were to have an idea that absolutely no one has even briefly toyed with before. When composer Sir Arthur Sullivan was accused of plagiarism he said 'We all have the same eight notes to work with'. Goethe said 'Everything worth thinking has been thought'.

And even if you were to have the best idea ever, you'd struggle to compete with the mother of all inventors – Mother Nature. Ideas we think were ours but Mother Nature got there first, include:

➤ Jet propulsion, which is used by the squid.

➤ The hypodermic needle, which is the principle used by the fangs of poisonous snakes to inject their venom.

➤ Radar, used by bats to hunt on the wing.

➤ Velcro, which is based on the burrs that clung to the trousers of Swiss Engineer George de Mestral when he went hunting in the forest.

➤ Have you ever noticed how when a sparrow glides, its body shape resembles that of a Harrier Jump Jet? Or perhaps that should be the other way around!

So, the world is full of great ideas. We should do the smart thing – and appropriate the best ones for ourselves. In case you're worrying about the legal issues raised by my exhortation to act like Dick Turpin – let me reassure you. The Copyright, Designs and Patents Act 1988 is not designed to stop the distribution of ideas. Copyright, under both UK law and the International Berne Convention is designed to protect the *expression* of ideas – that is, something that is created and then 'fixed' on paper, on film, tape or a digital medium such as a computer hard drive.

The type of works that copyright protects include original literary, dramatic or musical works, original artistic works, sound recordings, TV programmes, videos and so forth.

You cannot copyright a pure idea – and even the best brains in the world use this fact to help their creative thinking processes. Charles Darwin didn't single-handedly think up the notion of evolution, but shared the origination of the concept with Alfred Russel Wallace.

The UK not-for-profit sector has some interesting examples of organisations benefiting greatly from good ideas that have been developed first elsewhere. Take the Library Service. A number of libraries, such as 'The 'Idea Store' in Bow in East London, Bournemouth Library and Peckham Library, have borrowed the idea of coffee bars and chill-out areas from private sector book shops here and in the United States. This kind of thinking has helped them throw off the traditional and somewhat musty image associated with libraries of old and has led to relaxed, family-oriented places. These and a few other libraries up and down the country are currently bucking the trend of falling library use.

Case study: In 2003 Helen Mirren and Julie Walters starred in a movie called *Calendar Girls*. The film told the true story of the gutsy members of the Rylstone and District Women's Institute in Yorkshire who raised money for charity by baring all for a 'page 3 girl'-type calendar. Their exploits attracted such wide interest that the calendar grew from an initial print run of 500 to become the best-selling calendar of its year in the world! Later that year female staff at the Beacon Leisure Centre in Fife copied the idea to raise money for the Scottish Society of the Prevention of Cruelty to Animals.

Benchmarking

You can learn a tremendous amount by measuring your performance against that of other organisations. You can choose to do it with organisations which are similar to yours ('in-the-box' benchmarking) or agencies that are entirely dissimilar to yours ('out-of-the-box' benchmarking).

The following issues can all be benchmarked:

➤ fundraising practices and sources;

➤ management systems like appraisal or disciplinary procedures;

➤ monitoring and evaluation practices;

➤ salary levels;

➤ training policies and programmes;

➤ market research techniques;

➤ promotional materials (brochures, annual reports, etc.).

Out-of-the-box benchmarking could take you to charities dealing in entirely different fields, or even out of the sector altogether. For example we can learn much from the way businesses organise themselves.

Case study: In the pit lane of a Formula 1 Grand Prix there is a team of up to eight people. Everyone has their own job, from changing the tyres to cleaning the driver's visor and refuelling the car. The members of the team have to work in harmony. Decisions have to be made in an instant. Any mistakes could spell disaster. A London hospital looked at the way such teams worked together and learnt lessons for their resuscitation crash teams.

Formula 1 itself is not averse to learning from 'out-of-the-box' sources. The computerised launch control used on modern F1 cars was originally designed to launch US fighters from aircraft carrier flight decks!

Exercise 31

Do some benchmarking

Use a technique such as mind mining, radiant thinking or the fishbone technique to list things in your organisation that could be benchmarked.

Five ways to generate information

Marketing gurus Philip Kotler and Alan Andreasen suggest a number of practical techniques for generating information from outside your organisation, (30) including:

➤ Establishing a jointly funded clearinghouse to share ideas

➤ Regular scheduled visits or calls to other organisations to learn from them

➤ Someone taking on the responsibility of reading journals and magazines (including those that are specific to your business or sector and those that come from outside) and operating an in-house clipping service

➤ Regular attendance at conferences

➤ The direct solicitation of ideas from users/staff/funders etc. – rather than sitting and waiting for these.

The authors make the point that the 'idea manager' in an organisation should have some power, otherwise the ideas are likely to get squashed.

Create!

Exercise 32

Set your team a task. Ask each member of your team to collect the annual reports of at least five other charities or organisations similar to your own. Their task is to examine the annual reports paying particular attention to:

> the layout, design, use of colour, headlines, wording and overall impact

> the way the accounts are presented

> the way the opinions and quotes of third parties, such as celebrities, peer professionals or users are used to convince you that their work is of the highest quality

> the way they present their fundraising case and the ease with which the reader can contribute to any appeal

> the quality of the response (e.g. how quickly your competitor sent out its report, whether it sent the right information, what kind of letter was included, etc.)

> anything else that impresses you or otherwise!

Report back to each other after about a month (it will take that long to ask for these reports, receive them and analyse them).

What can you learn? What should you change about your own approach or processes? How can you get better next time?

Use a crystal ball (or the next best thing)

You must flexibly be prepared to deal with various possible futures.

Edward de Bono

Sometimes the world changes – and with it the future. Take the invention of the automobile. By the late nineteenth century, economic planners predicted that by 1940 Manhattan Island would be waist deep in horse manure, based on trends in population growth and horse ownership. They just didn't see the change, and the changed future that it brought.

And while we're on the subject of automobiles, take the case of Henry Ford. It is well known that Ford 'democratised' the automobile by producing the first mass-produced car – his Model T. In the process he pioneered the use of the production line for large-scale industrial manufacturing. This process would revolutionise industry and business across the world and it turned Ford Motors into one of America's largest corporations. Ford's famous catch phrase, 'you can have any colour, so long as it is black', summed up the no frills, straightforward approach that made him millions. What is less well known is that Henry Ford's insistence on sticking rigidly to the original Model T in the face of competition from other manufacturers brought his company to its knees. Wedded to what *had* been a very successful product design, he resisted all attempts by his advisors, (including his son Adsell) to offer a wider range of colours and designs. Despite selling over 15 million Model Ts, the company came very close to disappearing forever in the wake of competition from other manufacturers. Only when Adsell took over the business did its fortunes revive.

Why is this story relevant to a consideration of creative thinking? Well, it seems to me that Henry Ford would have been able to make better quality decisions if he had had a crystal ball. If only he had been able to look into the future, spot the changes in customer expectations and the emergence of competitors, then he might not have stuck so doggedly to a car design that had once worked, but was less suitable for a developing marketplace.

And the same thing surely is true for not-for-profit managers. If only we had a crystal ball to tell us which way the wind would blow tomorrow, then we could plan much more effectively. Well here is the rub. There is a simple tool available to you which, if not quite a crystal ball, is surely the next best thing.

STEP analysis

The management tool in question is called a STEP analysis, and it is used to measure trends and developments that are happening in the world at large. STEP is an acronym which stands for: **S**ocial, **T**echnological, **E**conomic and **P**olitical trends and developments.

Football legend Gary Lineker credits his success at scoring goals with an ability to gauge where the ball *will be*, not where the ball is. He became brilliant at guessing which space the ball would arrive in and he ran into that area to wait for it. Lots of organisations have got into trouble by being experts at running to where the ball is – but having no clue as to where it will be when they get there! Just like the position of the ball in a game of football, the outside world will change, either positively, or adversely, and this will impact on your organisation. The 'football' in this case represents funding trends, legislation, political developments and so forth and a STEP analysis is a very good way of tracking likely impacts. Thinking under the four headings described above is an effective way of identifying significant developments or trends in your external environment. You cannot influence these trends, you cannot prevent their impact, but you do need to be aware of them because they may define what is and what is not possible – the scope of your future activities. You need to take them into account in your planning. They may be very bad news – 'the government has changed its policy and less money will be available for organisations such as ourselves'. Or it might be good news – the New Opportunities Fund was great if you were in the business of technology, training and education.

Social

What are the key social trends?

> If you raise money for medical research, is it Alzheimer's, CJD or HIV or cancer that has the highest public profile? Currently, is your cause relatively popular or unpopular?

> If you run a youth project, how do young people spend their leisure time? Would they prefer outward bound courses or on-line gaming facilities?

Technological

What new technologies exist that change how you and similar organisations might offer services? Residential care was transformed by the 'bleeper' revolution which enabled old people to live in independent accommodation and yet be monitored by a mobile warden, armed with a pager which would send a message if an old person got into difficulties.

> What role are web pages playing in getting the message across? Is it enough to furnish a page with brochure ware or is truly interactive software the answer?

> Are you fully using the Internet? East London Business Alliance Forum e-mailed all of its member businesses to sell the idea of 'volunteering for charity' to their employees. Could you do something similar?

> What about future technological developments, such as the digital TV revolution which will soon bring the Internet to into everyone's living room, without the need for a computer? Are you prepared?

> At its annual conference in 2003 the Professional Association of Teachers discussed the idea that password-protected web cams could be set up in the classroom to allow parents to a) take a more active and interactive role in their children's education and b) help with disciplining unruly children.

Economic

> Will funder budgets be increased, decreased or stay the same?

> Is there growing competition for dwindling resources? Or are there exciting new opportunities which you will be well placed to take advantage of? When the director of a northern homelessness charity discovered that one of the country's biggest mortgage lenders was to set up a charitable foundation she was straight on the phone to the managing director of the bank to offer her help in assisting the foundation define its policy concerning the support of social housing organisations. Did she suggest that her organisation would make a good grant recipient? We can only speculate ...

> What is the state of the local economy? The Theatre by the Lake in Cumbria found that the foot and mouth epidemic in 2002, by bringing the local tourist economy to a standstill, was likely to bring down revenues significantly for all theatres and tourist attractions in the area.

Political

➤ If you work with the elderly, what is the government's agenda? Will resources be strategically directed towards frail or active elders?

➤ If you work with people with a disability, how will disability discrimination legislation affect you?

➤ Is political control likely to change at the level at which you work (local, regional, national)? How will this impact on you?

Will issues such as these change during the next three to five years or are they more likely to stay fixed?

Checklist

Remember that a STEP analysis is externally focused. Issues to consider usually include:

➤ changes in the law;

➤ changing social attitudes;

➤ changes in how people spend their money and time;

➤ changes in political policy or personnel;

➤ developments in stakeholder policies and plans;

➤ technical advances, whether mechanical, scientific, procedural, or intellectual;

➤ changes in the level or type of need;

➤ changes in the relative wealth of a target market segment;

➤ media opinion;

➤ changes in population or demography.

Case study: One technologically driven development of recent years has been the increasing number of people using the Internet to seek medical information and build virtual communication networks with others. A study conducted by the Boston Consulting Group demonstrated that four in every five on-line computer users in the US has searched for health-related information on the Internet. This trend prompted The Robert Wood Johnson Foundation in Princeton, New Jersey, to announce 18 grants totalling nearly five million dollars to support the use of low-cost, easy-access Internet software to improve health behaviour and disease management.

Exercise 33

Undertake a STEP analysis for your organisation. Remember that it is a bit like gazing into a crystal ball. You are looking for clues, suggestions or hints as to how the world will be, so that you can plan and act accordingly.

Step analysis

The social factors and trends which may affect my organisation are:

1 _____

_____

2 _____

_____

3 _____

_____

The technological factors and trends which may affect my organisation are:

1 _____

_____

2 _____

_____

3 _____

_____

The economic factors and trends which may affect my organisation are:

1 _____

_____

2 _____

_____

3 _____

_____

The political factors and trends which may affect my organisation are:

1 _____

_____

2 _____

_____

3 _____

_____

Now decide what you should do in order to avoid the **pitfalls** and **threats** described above. How can you take the **opportunities** presented?

Live a life unlimited

*If one advances confidently in the direction of one's dreams, and endeavours
to live the life which one has imagined, one will meet with a success unexpected
in common hours.*

Henry David Thoreau

First, seek to believe

The techniques in this book are designed help you in your quest for greater levels
of creativity. Some show you how to withhold judgement and tolerate ambiguity.
Some demonstrate practical techniques to avoid the adoption of positions and to
break established patterns in search of new ways of doing things.

But before, during and after reading this book, you'll also need to do some work
on the only tool you have to help you think creatively in the long term – your
brain. Remember that creativity equals …

Changed thinking leading to changed action

The first stage in becoming more creative is to accept that you have it within you to
be fantastically creative. But don't worry, that's not in fact as hard as it may sound.
In fact you already are an expert. Let me explain. By being born, you changed the
world. Really – since you arrived, it has never been quite the same place. Clearly
you changed the lives of your parents (quite dramatically, I'm sure!). But since that
time, you have also gone through life making constant little ripples. Every
conversation you have ever had, piece of advice you've offered or argument you've
taken part in has changed something. Every friend you've ever made or person
you've helped out is grateful for the fact of your existence. In fact every person
you've ever met and left an impression on will never be quite the same again!

Now they don't realise it at the time. When you make a cup of coffee for a colleague
they don't wait until you've left the room, go all misty eyed and murmur 'I thank God
that she was born!'. But your influence has nevertheless changed something at that
moment, and it is much more than providing caffeine for an overworked colleague!

Think of it this way. A popular way of describing chaos theory is that if a butterfly
flaps its wings in Argentina, this could eventually produce a hurricane in London.
Everyday you flap butterfly wings a hundred different times in a hundred
different ways and the world is changed forever as a result. You go through each
day making ripples, or eddies, in other people's lives – and these are cumulative.
The sum total of these ripples every year is, frankly, enormous!

But most of the time, (if you're like most people) you don't see it. We tend not to
recognise the impact that we have. We don't know that we've changed everything.
*And as a result it is easy to believe that we do not have the power to make change
happen.* People believe in the fates, in astrology, in the power of the state, in the

wisdom of others, in the class system, in the education system, in religion, in the economy, politics, organisational procedures, standards, values, in anything it seems – but themselves. We go through much of life taking things for granted, believing that things get done in a certain way because that is the 'right way'. What we mean is that it is the 'accepted' way – but that does not mean that it is the best way. Our mind set, much of the time, is one of unquestioning acceptance of the structures that surround us. Is that appropriate for someone who from the moment they were born has been dramatically altering the world? Surely a more appropriate mind set would be one that said 'I am an agent of change. It doesn't have to be this way even if everyone else thinks so. It's my job to question whether things have to stay the same'.

So here is my challenge to you and it comes in three parts:

1   Believe that you have already changed everything – *because you have*.

2   Reject the thinking that says because something 'is', therefore it 'must be' – *because it needn't*.

3   Believe that you have the power to continue to change anything – *because you do*.

Step beyond limited thinking

Look again at the quote from Henry Thoreau above. He is saying that you must dare to believe in your dreams – and that if you do, you will be astonished at what you achieve. The formula for achievement appears to be simple. Just believe that you will succeed and you will.

By the same token, the formula for underachievement seems equally clear. Here it is:

1   *Don't* dream.

2   *Don't* believe that you can change anything and do anything, if you put your mind to it.

3   *Do* believe that you're not very creative and that other people have the best ideas.

Limited thinking places constraints not just in terms of our own ability to be creative, but in lots of other ways too. For example:

➤   If you believe that everybody is basically out for themselves, you'll never really trust another person. If so, you're unlikely to enjoy the full trust of another.

➤   If you believe that funders are becoming harder to satisfy, you'll struggle to satisfy them.

➤   If you believe that the management committee doesn't really understand the work, then you'll fail to develop the capacity to describe it to them.

When I talk about life unlimited, what I mean is, give yourself the freedom to dream. Think unlimited thoughts about:

➤   what you can achieve;

➤   how you can transform your organisation;

➤   how to tackle problems, because they are never intractable.

See beyond the artificial constraints imposed by limited thinking and picture 'the possible' in full technicolor. As President John F. Kennedy once said, 'The *problems* of the world cannot possibly be solved by sceptics or cynics whose horizons are limited by the obvious realities. We need men who can dream of things that never were'. I think he meant to say 'men and women', but apart from that – he was spot on!

What causes limited thinking?

Think back to your childhood. Can you remember many occasions when your parents, teachers or peers said 'you are incredible' 'that was brilliant' or even 'I love you'? Take a second to consider how many instances of positive reinforcement such as these you can recall. Now think about the times teachers, parents or peers made you feel slow, unattractive, foolish, unimportant and so on.

If the former outweigh the latter in your consciousness that is wonderful as you have been given a tremendous gift. However, the chances are you can recall the negative episodes with greater clarity and detail. Maybe the pain caused still hurts a little. This isn't necessarily because there really were many more such instances – and it is *certainly* not because you are inadequate in any way – it is because negative reinforcement is so much more powerful for most people. We need to be accepted and loved. Any words or actions which appear to undermine this leave an indelible impression. And that impression can impact on how we carry our thinking over into adulthood. It can lead to a tendency to set sights low or assume that 'I can't do that', 'that's never going to happen', or 'that would be nice but it's not very likely'. The more that these and similar disempowering phrases are repeated over the years, the more it appears that they are true. Well they're not!

The lexicon of limitation

Stop that!	Don't even think about it	Don't be silly/stupid/ridiculous
You can't do that	Oh questions, questions, questions!	It'll never work
No!	When will you ever learn?	Stick to what you're good at

Imagined hindsight

This is a practical technique designed to help you break free from any limitations in your thinking. It has five key stages.

1 First of all picture a problem (professional or personal; people or practically oriented).

2 Now, rather than try to solve that problem – simply travel into the future and visualise how life will be when you have solved it. So for example, if your team is quite low on morale, conflict is high or unresolved and work is quite a stressful place to be at the moment – imagine your team, at some point in the future happy, motivated, effective, pulling together and experiencing the synergy of effective teamwork – a group of people whose whole is greater

than the sum of the parts. It is important that you really work on this vision. Consider the detail. Imagine 'real' situations that have 'happened' as a result of this fantastic teamwork. Consider carefully all aspects of the benefits that accrue – the implications for the organisation as a whole, your own state of mind, the quality of the work. Don't say 'this is what will happen'. Remember that you have travelled to the future and it already has happened. So express these details in the present tense by saying 'this is how it does happen now'.

3 Now 'remember', using imagined hindsight, all the things that you had to do to create this happy and functioning team. You will remember the team building exercises, away days, training programmes, quiet chats and nights out that led to this blissfully functioning group of people.

4 Come back into the present.

5 Create a plan to make all of the things on your list happen in real time.

The advantages of this approach are:

➤ It stops your critical left brain chiming in with 'we can't do that because ...' or 'that'll never work because ...'. These are typical left-brain responses to right-brain creativity – which invariably result in the death of ideas before they've had a chance to mature or develop.

➤ Because it eliminates the 'sensible' blocks imposed by the left brain, you can get to a picture of what is possible that otherwise you'd have abandoned at an earlier stage. You will give yourself the space to create your dream.

➤ Once you have your dream, you can move towards it. The technique helps you identify the small steps that together represent the completion of a challenging journey.

➤ There is a good deal of evidence which suggests that the part of our brain which deals with emotions cannot tell the difference between a real event and a powerfully imagined event (that's why horror movies really scare you). If you create a very clear visualised picture, then your brain will begin to believe that it is possible and act accordingly. Your confidence, commitment and self-belief will, quite magically, rise. You will find that you develop the emotional and mental resources to put your plan into action.

Exercise 34

1 Choose your problem.

2 Travel into the future and create your 'life unlimited' picture.

3 Now 'remember' the actions you took to bring this picture about.

4 Come back to the present and create your plan.

Toy with the problem

All men and women were born creative – we were all children once.

Sidney Shore

If we were to use a technique described elsewhere in this book – random triggers – and start with the word 'Toy' you might end up with a list something like this:

➤ to play with

➤ to break

➤ to imagine.

That's a good list to trigger some thoughts on how toying with a problem can help us solve it!

The importance of play

Children can make a game of anything. Toddlers love to join in with tidying up or washing the car. Lots of play is imaginative and based on role modelling – mums and dads, doctors and nurses, heroes and villains. This turning of everyday activity into play is an essential method of discovering how the world and what it contains works. On one level play works as a tool to develop creativity because it is all about exploring, finding out and learning. On a deeper level play helps to break down the barriers between categories and concepts that the systematic and logical left brain creates to make sense of the world. When we are relaxed and playful our intuitive right brain is fired up to help us see the bigger picture, and begins to connect distant or unrelated ideas.

Breaking toys

Most toys end up broken or damaged eventually. The ones that survive probably haven't been played with much! The destruction of toys is often an essential part of finding out how they work. 'Let's see what's inside here'; 'What will happen if I pull that off?' etc. Can you pull the problem apart, or slice it up in some way? Remember what we said earlier about pyramid thinking or using the fishbone technique to break problems down into their constituent parts? Can you trial a solution, in the way a toddler might 'suck it and see' to discover more about a new toy?

Use imagination

Children use their imagination extensively when they play. Now you may think of the real world and the world of the imagination as being two separate things, but the latest research into brain function would suggest otherwise. Put simply, there is a blurring between the two. The theory goes like this:

1 When we experience something, electrical impulses leap from neurone to neurone across the surface of our brain, creating a pathway. These pathways become the architecture of our memory, emotions, thoughts, feelings and actions.

2 These pathways are reinforced the more times we undergo the experience. This helps us learn. Eventually the pathway becomes ingrained – and it becomes natural for us to react in a certain way when presented with any specific situation. The pathways make up a sort of operating code for our mind. When we laugh in response to humour, feel fear at the thought of pain, learn to walk or run or talk or chew, grow more adept at riding a bike or driving a car – what is really happening is that a certain pathway between certain brain cells is becoming more and more established. This is, quite simply, why practice makes perfect.

3 Now it gets interesting! As we have recently noted, your subconscious mind cannot distinguish real and imagined experience. This means it is almost as useful to repeatedly imagine something as it is to repeatedly undergo the real experience. In either case, the impulses leap down the familiar path and the path becomes more deeply ingrained.

The most powerful form of imagining for most people is visualisation. That is because most people interpret the world primarily (though not exclusively) via the sense of sight.

What the brain function analysis described above tells us is that repeated visualisation is akin to a sort of mental practice that has the same benefit as real practice in terms of teaching your brain how to achieve something.

Repeated visualisation in action

Formula 1 racing driver David Coulthard can be observed before a race, sitting in his cockpit of his car, hands over his eyes, visualising every turn and bend of the track that awaits him. It has been proven that this process increases his reaction times during the real race.

A group of basketball players were split into three by researchers at the University of Chicago. Group 1 was asked to practise shooting into the net for three weeks. The second group was barred from any practice at all. The third group was encouraged to practise by using visualisation only – they never went near a real basketball. At the end of the three-week period they were given balls and asked to demonstrate their abilities. The results were astonishing. The group that had really practised showed an improved shooting ability of 24%. The group that hadn't practised at all showed no improvement at all. The third group who had used only visualisation improved their shooting scores by 23%! (31)

Exercise 35

Choose your problem and play with it as a child would. This might include:

> **Examining it from all angles:** e.g. What do other people think? What would happen if you undertook course of action 'A'? Or if you undertook course of action 'B'?

> **Taking it apart:** Can you break the problem down into its constituent parts? How do they fit together? What has gone wrong?

> **Attempting repair:** Can you take out the broken part – and will it still work? Can you remove the broken part without disturbing the rest of the mechanism? Do you need to take it to a specialist toy repair shop?

> **Sucking it to see:** Can you try various resolutions to the problem as 'pilots' without committing to a permanent course until you've had a chance to monitor results?

Can you visualise what needs to be done? Can you mentally practise taking action and imagine the consequences?

Schedule creativity into your day

People tend to be at their creative best at different times of the day. Some of us are 'early birds' others 'night owls'. If you are serious about creativity, then it makes sense to think about creating a schedule which allows you to do creative work when you are at your most energetic, alert and focused.

Exercise 36

Try this four-step approach to scheduling in creativity

1 Ask yourself 'When am I at my best mentally: morning, afternoon or evening?'

2 Find a slot, even if it is just 30 minutes each week, to schedule in some creative work or creative thinking. Block out this time in your diary

3 Pick one of the techniques described in this book – any will do – so long as you are comfortable with it and try it when your creativity slot comes around.

Remember that your environment, your colleagues and your boss will all impact on your ability to be creative during your creativity slot. So manage them as best you can. You might do solo work in your creativity refuge, or you could organise an ideas generating session with colleagues at an optimum time.

Business process re-engineering

This technique involves stripping the issues back to fundamentals and asking very basic questions to arrive at the best way forward. It is about redesigning processes and structures from first principles. The questions are always simple and sometimes, as you will see, a little scary. They include:

> 'Why do we do this at all?'

> 'Why do we do this in this particular way?'

> 'Are there better ways of doing it?'

> 'Are there faster ways of doing it?'

> 'Are there cheaper ways of doing it?'

It's the implications of these simple questions that are scary, because they lead to answers such as:

> 'We are probably not *really* meeting *all* the needs of the people we are here to help.'

> 'We should be thinking about making redundancies.'

> 'We should close project 'A' and concentrate on project 'B'.'

> 'We should try to put a new board of trustees in place.

The process is about being honest about the blocks and obstacles in your way, imagining what you would do if you could start again with a blank sheet, and taking whatever action is required to move from the current problematic reality to the future, better alternative.

Case study: Guide Dogs for the Blind was founded in 1934. The mission of the organisation has always been to give mobility and independence to visually impaired people. In 1934, providing a guide dog was just about the only (and certainly the best) way to do this. By the latter part of the twentieth century however, society, the needs of blind people and the employable technologies had all changed significantly. Chair of the charity, Barry Weatherill, stated in 2002 'This has been the year in which Guide Dogs has embraced the challenge of re-shaping and improving our services for the future'. (32) The charity had effectively re-engineered its contribution to the lives of visually impaired people by (among other things) campaigning to ensure that guide dog owners would never be refused access to a taxi or minicab, working towards tighter firework controls and ensuring greater levels of consultation.

To summarise ...

Being creative is more about attitude than aptitude. The more you practise the better you will become. The focus of this section has been more about an intellectual 'lifestyle change' to help build your personal capacity to be creative, rather than a focus on solving specific problems.

Here is a checklist of actions you can take:

1 New experiences can help you see things with new eyes. Seek them out.

2 Try to be a 'contrarian'. Look for accepted custom and practice and ask – 'why?', or 'what if?'

3 Spot your own habits and break them. Sit in a different seat. Do things at different times, in different places, with different people.

4 Switch off the chattering left brain from time to time. Allow space for bits of the submerged iceberg to break off and float to the surface.

5 Sleep on it. Don't be hasty.

6 Study, take your time, contemplate. Study some more.

7 Notice your psychological state when you are in a 'zone' of creativity. Notice your environment at the same time. Try to replicate then when you need to 'switch on' creativity.

8 Hang around with people who are inspirational. Remember that almost everyone is inspirational if you really observe and listen.

9 Look around you and pick up new ideas from wherever you can.

10 If you are mentally more alert in the morning, schedule in the tasks that need high levels of creativity then. Take charge of your day.

11 Toy with issues. Do what Melvyn Bragg has called 'rummaging around' with ideas.

12 Go back to basics, re-engineer it. Ask 'why?', 'how?', 'what if?'.

Your FIFTH challenge is to believe that you are creative and then act accordingly. You can either *think* your way into *acting* creatively or you can *act* your way into *thinking* creatively. It is a circle – it doesn't matter where you start the process. The key thing is simply to believe – and go for it.

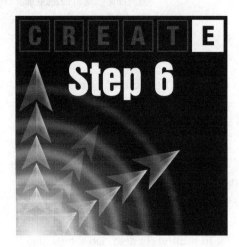

Step 6

Encourage ...

... others. Build a creativity culture

Why 'encourage'?

Consider the language of management: 'systems', 'procedure', 'plan', 'policy', 'analysis', 'projection' – all these words suggest a mind set which is about:

> needing to know what will come next;

> feeling uncomfortable with any gaps in certainty;

> making assumptions to fill those gaps.

Of course, it is important that managers do have information to inform their decision making. Of course we need to get everyone singing to the same sheet, in order to coordinate our activities and make sure that our teams or organisations are effective. But if we approach our work with conceptualisations regarding roles, systems and structures that are overly rigid, if we do things today a certain way, because that's the way they were done yesterday, then we run the risk of killing creativity before it gets a chance to flourish. We create a culture which is anathamatic to the freedom of expression which creativity demands.

Luckily however, it is also possible to do just the opposite – and create a culture which values, stimulates and nurtures creativity.

Section overview

In this section we shall look at some methods to help build a creativity culture in your team or organisation. Specifically, you will learn to:

> build cooperative problem-solving practices

> trust one another's judgement

> create a questioning, as opposed to complacent culture in your organisation

> discover how to motivate creativity

> look at a range of ways to encourage people to take risks with their thinking.

Avoid blaming others

The Buck Stops Here.

Harry S.Truman

Blame gets us nowhere. As soon as you blame someone for a failure, or because something didn't happen, or because a problem hasn't been solved, a number of things almost inevitably happen:

> ➤ It becomes personal. The focus stops being on the issue, and starts to be concerned with the people involved.

> ➤ You get denial. You blame, they deny it, before long no one is listening to anyone else. Everyone's trying to shift the blame.

> ➤ You lose cooperation. In a 'blame culture' people tend not to trust one another. They are too busy watching their backs. And when that happens, they're not likely to cooperate.

A simple way to avoid 'blame culture'

When something goes wrong, and you have to meet with others to sort it out, the avoidance of a simple phrase and the substitution of another can bring about a marked difference in the atmosphere.

The phrase to avoid is: 'OK, what went wrong?'.

You have to avoid this because people will tend to hear something different, such as 'OK, what did you do wrong?', or 'OK, describe how you failed'. No matter which way you look at it, 'wrong' has negative connotations, and strong associations with 'stupid', 'useless' and 'inadequate'.

The phrase you should use instead is: 'OK, what have we learned?'.

This has the advantage of using positive language. Implicit is the idea of moving on, not dwelling on the mistakes of the past, but using them to grow, develop and make sure that things improve. The preposition 'we' suggests a shared ownership of both the problem and the invaluable lesson that has been learned.

Working together – 10 tips for success

Many of the techniques in this book assume a group of people working together. However for that to work effectively, you might like to consider the following groundrules:

1 **Build trust.** Remember that the risk of failure is an essential part of developing creativity. For it to happen in any sort of team context, there must first exist trust. So confidentiality becomes very important.

2 **Keep it fun.** Adults can use their right brain best when they are not bored witless. Keep the energy high and insert serious amounts of fun into the business.

3   **Watch your language.** Language is the code we use to express our thought process. Try to catch yourself saying 'it will never work' – and change it to 'how can we make it work?'. Avoid the list of limited thinking phrases and words shown on page 107.

4   **Use a rapporter** to capture thought, ideas, whimsies, jokes. Better still tape the session and give everyone a tape to listen to in their car.

5   **Switch roles.** If one person tends to chair or lead the group, make sure that they step aside for the creative sessions. If you are the boss, take a back-seat role as far as possible in the planning of the session.

6   **Watch the process.** Try to keep an eye on the process. It's easy to slip off track, to find that you've drifted into 'critical-thinking' mode when everyone else is in 'idea-generation' mode. Some creative thinking teachers, such as Edward de Bono, say that you should appoint someone to sit 'outside of the thinking' to watch the process, and gently remind people to start applying the creativity rules again if they temporarily forget.

7   **Hold your session in a neutral venue.** People will associate familiar environments with familiar feelings and behaviours. If they are used to falling into a gentle slumber in the room where you hold your staff meetings, then that's what they'll do during a creative session held in the same room. So find a new environment, away from the usual associations and distractions. If the session concerns a really important issue, such as the mission of the organisation or new ideas to generate funding or the restructuring of projects and teams, go outside your organisation altogether. Can you stretch to a venue that will provide nicer biscuits and a view? It all helps people to relax and focus on the day.

> **Case study:** The Lawnmowers is a theatre company working with people with learning difficulties. The staff and trustees regularly book a day out of the office, preferably out of town, to discuss progress and generate ideas regarding the strategic plan, fundraising activities and the company's front-line work. Participants all agree that changing scene is a great boost to the quality of the thinking that takes place.

8   **Avoid 'right' or 'wrong' labels.** At the beginning of the session remind people that there are no right or wrong answers, that generating ideas is different from critically evaluating and that there will be room during the session for both. These will be kept quite separate of course.

9   **Begin by warming up.** I use what I call 'cereberobics' to help people limber up mentally. The cereberobic exercises are designed to:

> ➤ get the creative juices flowing;

> ➤ engage both left and right brains;

> ➤ let people begin to enjoy themselves;

You'll find some suggested cereberobics in Exercise 37 opposite.

10 **Celebrate**. When you've completed your session you should consider that you've taken risks, moved out on a limb, and gone that extra mile to find the best solution. In the process you've probably controlled your ego, bonded your team and had a laugh. You've really worked much harder than most do in the search for excellence. Have some chocolate. Go on. Oh go *on*!

Exercise 37

Cereberobics

Use mind mining (page 44) or radiant thinking techniques (page 46) to complete the following cereberobics:

1   Your boss arrives at work and responds to all attempts to engage him in conversation with the single word 'flartybart'. His conversation is as animated and tonally rich as usual – it's just that it consists of this one word only. What happened to him on his way to work?

_____

_____

_____

_____

_____

2   The government solves the housing crisis for young professional key workers by setting aside reservations in Wales and the Lake District. You will be restricted to these reservations as Native Americans once were, selling your skills via the Internet. You will live in a teepee. List all the advantages and disadvantages of this arrangement.

_____

_____

_____

_____

_____

3   On holiday you are overcome with a powerful urge to eat something hot and spicy. You enter a restaurant but can't understand the menu or speak the language. The waiter comes. List five ways you can successfully get the meal you want.

_____

_____

_____

_____

_____

Be a pain ... and feel the pain

Encourage heresy.

Carl Sagan

To cut a rather long philosophical story short, Nietzsche once said that strong and mature societies would eventually, and inevitably, become comfortable, complacent, set in their ways and unable therefore to adapt to change. They would then, inexorably, fall into decline. Into these societies occasionally there will come a visionary, able to see beyond the cage of habit and limited thinking and 'old' ways of doing things. These people are invariably seen as 'right royal pains in the extremities' by those who have a vested interest in doing things the old comfortable way. For example, Jesus Christ was a bit unpopular with the Pharisees because he was a friend of the poor, V.I. Lenin was definitely unbeloved of the Romanovs because he envisaged a new style of politics, Socrates was executed because he asked too many questions.

This is what Sidney Shore calls 'constructive discontent'. (33)

So what is the lesson? Take a leaf out of the book of the 'troublemakers' I've just listed and be difficult. Play devil's advocate, question attitudes and assumptions, try and stir them up. You don't have to have rows and fights with all your colleagues and friends. But you can gently offer questions instead of unthinking acquiescence. At all costs seek to avoid what has been labeled 'group think'. In a group think culture any thinking which does not support the preconceived ideas of the group is seen as heresy. Dissenters are seen as no longer 'one of us' and their views are ignored. You should also avoid a related phenomenon which I call 'nice think'. Nice think happens when a group of people are very concerned with being nice to each other and therefore fail to challenge the views of others in the group. Consensus tends to settle in a safe, middle ground and radical options are never put forward.

This approach cuts both ways of course. It's no good being a pain concerning the thinking of others if you can't handle being treated the same way. If you dish it out, you have to be prepared to take it. As Professor Dorothy Leonard of the Harvard Business School says, 'If you want an innovative organisation, you need to hire, work with and promote people who make you uncomfortable'. Not because they dribble down their chin during staff meetings (although I have worked with one or two of those) but because they challenge your assumptions and firmly held convictions.

Exercise 38

List below the people in your organisation or team who:

➤ usually see things the same way you do
➤ usually see things differently from you.

You'll recognise the former group because they will make you feel relaxed, you will find their company easy, you will agree a lot of the time and disagree rarely. The latter group will include people with whom you have the opposite experience. They will rub you up the wrong way. Their values may appear different to yours. They will approach problems in different ways. You may see the big picture while they get snagged on the detail (or vice versa). You may be optimistic while they are overly cautious (or vice versa) and so on.

People who think like me   People who don't

_____   _____
_____   _____
_____   _____
_____   _____

Now consider how you can involve those with whom you are not so comfortable in a problem-solving context, e.g. discussion group/sub-committee/informal consultation, etc.

Three cornerstones of creative thinking

Dr Teresa Amabile, Professor of Business Administration at the Harvard Business School, describes the 'Three Components of Creativity'. Writing in the *Harvard Business Review*, she considers how expertise, creative thinking skills and motivation are all required if creativity is to take place within structured organisations. (34)

1. Expertise

Expertise, in her model, is not just that connected to a person's current post or job. It also refers to all of the knowledge and experience that that person has gained in life. So a chief executive may also bring skills garnered from being a mother, a youth leader or a hockey player.

2. Creative thinking

Amabile includes in her description of creative thinking many of the elements listed elsewhere in this book. For example she cites a 'capacity to put existing ideas in new combinations', 'perseverance', 'the capacity for incubation' and the combination of 'knowledge from seemingly disparate fields'.

3. Motivation

Motivation is the fuel that drives the vehicle provided by the two elements listed above. All the expertise and ability to think creatively in the world will be useless if the person is not motivated to put them to good use.

In most organisations, there is a wealth of talent, both visible and hidden among the staff and volunteers. The ability to think creatively can be learned or encouraged by reading books like this one, or attending training courses. But nurturing a positive motivation to be creative among its people is the one element that most organisations leave out. And a car without fuel is going nowhere.

How to motivate creativity

There are three things a manager can do to build individual motivation to solve problems.

1 **Match people with the right task.** If you play to people's strengths you may find that they begin to enjoy the challenge. It seems obvious, but when we want to deliver a presentation, how many times do we see the person with the strongest dread of presenting being chosen? If a piece has to be written for the community newsletter, do we choose the best communicator, or simply the person who is closest to the task, to prepare the copy? If we do not put conscious effort into the matching process, then mismatches are inevitable. And then of course, we will have people who are not enthusiastic and engaged, far less passionate, about their task.

2 **Give people freedom to act.** A manager may give team members a clear brief, or target. But if the manager then constrains their freedom to act in order to retain control over how something is to be achieved, then they will limit the team's ability to provide creative solutions. So delegate responsibility for the results, as well as the task in hand. Ask people to solve the problem or to come back to you with alternative solutions, but not with problems. Hand over ownership of the problem. Light the blue touch paper of your people's creativity and then stand back.

3 **Give people time.** People need time to be creative. They need strategic time. In other words a long period of time in which to consider, gestate, ponder and wait for their subconscious brain or intuition to kick in. You don't necessarily get creativity by demanding results yesterday. They also need tactical time. This is time knitted into the fabric of a day to brainstorm or dream. So create a long enough timeline, but also encourage people to schedule in quiet time into their daily schedules. Encourage them to clear their decks of urgent but not necessarily important tasks and 'have a meeting with their creativity'.

Demand ideas

Nothing is more dangerous than an idea when it's the only one you have.

Emile Chartier

We can take a lesson from history. During the Second World War three of the combatant leaders displayed markedly different approaches to dealing with the ventured opinion of others. Hitler would fly into a rage if one of his generals offered a point of view that was not his own. Stalin welcomed advice from his general staff, but rewarded them with a firing squad if the ideas didn't work. Churchill, too, initially exerted a domineering personality and began to persuade his military advisors that they had better agree if they wanted their careers to flourish. He changed his approach, however, after his wife Clementine helped him realise that if he continued to be contemptuous of the ideas of others, 'presently, no ideas, good or bad will be forthcoming'.

So, it makes sense to celebrate ideas, whether they are good or bad. That's easy to say – but more challenging to accomplish. In fact, as we've mentioned before – we tend to be rather good at squashing ideas before they have had much of a chance to develop. As so often is the case, a metaphor from nature might help to focus your mind on the issue. It is impossible to judge just how strong and tall an oak tree will stand by looking at the acorn. An acorn is all potential. But to achieve its potential, it must be nurtured, protected and encouraged. It will need copious amounts of sunlight and rain to sprout green shoots. These shoots then need a bit of luck to get through their infancy without being eaten or trodden on. Only after a significant amount of time will anything that begins to resemble an oak tree take shape – and even then it will remain vulnerable for years to come. Ideas, though of course operating on a shorter timeline than oak trees, have the same challenges. They must:

➤ be allowed to germinate;

➤ be encouraged to grow.

➤ be protected from the elements (in the case of an oak's green shoots, the frost; in the case of ideas, scepticism, busyness, procedure and a host of other environmental factors).

For these three challenges to be successfully met it is not enough to say 'all ideas are welcomed'. Rather, it is necessary to work actively to encourage ideas and support them in their early stages of life.

Case study: The following list was produced in a seminar by delegates from Voluntary Action Westminster:

➤ communal lunches	➤ blue-sky time	➤ an ideas book
➤ yoga sessions	➤ Wednesday afternoon 'fun hour'	➤ team hugs
➤ a 'doodle wall'	➤ mad idea of the month	➤ fancy dress Friday

Although each of the above ideas has its own merits, I particularly liked the idea of a 'doodle wall': basically the idea suggests that one wall in your office is painted white. Preferably, the wall should be clear and flat, free of windows, radiators or other obstructions. Effectively it is a canvas. People can doodle on it as they search for inspiration. When it is finally full of charts, drawings, arrows, shapes, lists, etc., you simply paint over it and start again.

Create!

Exercise 39

Encourage ideas

In the space below, list some of the ways in which you might be able to encourage ideas from your staff. Remember, the 'stupider' the better, because creativity is about generating, generating, generating, and only then choosing.

_____

_____

_____

_____

_____

_____

Set an idea quota

The CIA is said to establish idea quotas for its employees. The quality is much less important than the quantity. What counts is to get people into the habit of thinking. As George Bernard Shaw said, 'few people think more than two or three times a year. I've made an international reputation for myself by thinking once or twice a week'.

Exercise 40

Encourage more ideas

In the space below, list some of the ways in which you might be able to encourage ideas from someone you know who may feel particularly non-creative. Visualise this person. Focus on them. Which techniques would be particularly appropriate for them? Come up with an action plan below:

_____

_____

Think like a warrior goddess

Business strategist Charles Handy likens management styles to Greek gods. (35) Athena was an action-oriented warrior goddess. Athena model teams have a proactive, action-focused problem-solving approach. They tend to be non-hierarchical, flexible and 'competence' based, rather than 'role' based. If you have a specific problem, you can put an Athenian task group or project team together and ask them to solve it.

Design your task group for success

A successful task group is likely to have three key features. It will be:

1 **Designed.** It is important to select the right personnel to ensure success. As any B movie fan will tell you, a successful criminal mob must include the following characters: brains (for the thinking), fingers (for the safe-cracking), muscles (for the rough stuff) and a good getaway driver. Your task group should be designed to bring a wide range of experience, backgrounds, skills and outlooks to the challenge. The last thing you want is to have a group of people who will share the same attitudes, opinions and approaches!

2 **Supportive.** Our purpose in bringing a disparate group of individuals together is to provide a creative frisson – not to allow them to argue about who knows best or who has the 'best' approach. So it is vitally important that the members of the group want to support each other, share a common purpose, recognise that each brings something different to the table and see the key goal as solving the problem, rather than winning any arguments that may occur.

3 **Empowered.** A successful task group must feel that it has the resources to get the job done. These should include the freedom to meet, the ability to spend time together, and information about how much, if any, money is available. Management should empower the group by authorising the use of all these resources before the group starts its thinking.

> **Case study:** A charity supporting people with mental health challenges in the Midlands needed to produce a marketing strategy to get the message across that it was professional and that its services would deliver the outcomes required by potential customers, such as the local authority. The organisation didn't have a full time PR or marketing officer, so it pulled together a task group to handle the work. Members of the group came from within the senior management team, middle management and front-line workers. One was chosen because of her chairing ability, another because he was skilled at writing copy; another because of contacts in the statutory agencies, yet another because she had detailed knowledge of all of the charity's services. When the strategy was delivered and implementation had begun, the task group was disbanded.

Give and ye shall receive

Give away everything you know, and more will come back to you.

Paul Arden

It is said that if you spend all day giving out smiles, you'll get twice as many back. The same could be said of ideas. Despite this, there are organisations where people hang on to their ideas in case anyone else gets the credit. If you jealously guard your ideas, then you contribute to an anti-ideas culture (an idea only really becomes alive when it is shared). If on the other hand you share your ideas readily, then you contribute to an intellectually open culture, where ideas can breathe and flourish. Remember, you cannot copyright ideas. They don't belong to you. You're just looking after them for everyone else until they're strong enough to survive on their own.

So have lots of ideas. Remember that most will be rubbish. Share them widely. Keep a sense of humour.

Exercise 41

Sharing strategies

In the space below, list ideas from this book (or indeed, any other source) for sharing ideas more effectively within your team or organisation.

_____

_____

_____

Prepare for resistance

What progress we are making. In the Middle Ages they would have burned me. Now they are content with burning my books.

Sigmund Freud

People don't like change. And they really don't like significant change. When Nye Bevan was given the job of creating the National Health Service in 1945 he did it in the face of fierce opposition from those with interests in the maintenance of the status quo. The Church of England is currently struggling with the issue of women clergy. However that one is resolved, massive numbers of people will be left disillusioned and upset.

So let's be clear. If your creative thinking results in significant change you can be sure that people will both resent and resist it. And as the quote from Freud above illustrates, this resistance may be explicit and explosive, or more subtle. Either they will burn your books – in other words trash your idea – or they may 'burn' you, by attacking your integrity or credibility!

So be strong – and keep your course fixed. You know that you are on the right path!

To summarise …

Socrates was executed because of the questions he asked, Copernicus threatened with excommunication for his theories and Edison laughed at on the floor of Congress regarding his idea for the telephone. 'What are you going to do Mr Edison – put one in every town in the country?' You will fare much better as a creative thinker if you are not the only original thinker in your team, department or organisation, but instead work in a culture of creativity.

To ensure that this is so work on:

1 Avoiding blame. Don't ask 'who is to blame?' Ask 'what have we learned?'

2 Work with, hire and promote the people who ask questions.

3 Give people the freedom to act and make mistakes.

4 Match people with tasks that suit them and their special talents.

5 Make it clear that ideas are good. Demand them.

6 Try new things and give them the space and time to grow. An acorn is all potential and its green shoot will need a lot of nurturing if it is to become an oak.

The FINAL challenge in this book is to challenge your colleagues, to take them with you, to change the way things are done. It will at times seem hard – but remember that great things can be achieved by a group of people who bring cooperation, trust, motivation and a lack of fear to their endeavours. In fact few great things have ever been created unless this is so.

Action plan

If you don't act on your creative thoughts – your creativity is dead.

Floyd Hurt

At the beginning of this book I shared with you my definition of creativity, 'changed thinking, leading to changed action'.

Well, you've read the book and had time to consider whether it has changed your thinking. Now it is time to decide on the action!

Remember the CREATE programme. The techniques in the programme are:

 CONFIRM and establish the real problem.

 Take **R**ISKs because security and creativity are incompatible.

 EXPAND the number of options and potential solutions available.

 ANALYSE – use critical thinking to select the best solution.

 Develop techniques to help you to **T**HINK more productively.

 ENCOURAGE others and build a creativity culture.

Exercise 42

In the box below plot your creativity enhancement plan.

Techniques we could use	Problem/circumstance/issue	People involved

Further reading

Creativity and problem solving

Von Oech, Roger   *A Whack on the Side of the Head*
(Thorsons 1990)
A seminal book on creative thinking.
An excellent introduction to the topic.

Higgins, James M.   *101 Creative Problem Solving Techniques*
(The New Management Publishing Company 1994)
A great and versatile toolkit.

Epstein, Dr Robert   *Creativity Games for Trainers* (McGraw-Hill 1996)
Interesting and fun. Especially good for group work.

Koestler, Arthur   *The Act of Creation* (Hutchison 1964)
For the serious student of creativity only!

Buzan, Tony   *The Power of Creative Intelligence* (Thorsons 2001)
Buzan writes not just intelligently but entertainingly.

Buzan, Tony   *How to Mind Map* (Thorsons 2002)
A definitive description of this powerful tool
by its originator.

McCoy, Charles   *Why Didn't I Think of That?* (Prentice Hall 2002)
A perspective from the USA. Good on both left-
and right-brain methods.

Adair, John   *Decision Making and Problem Solving* (CIPD 1997)
An interesting book which places much emphasis
on left-brain, systematic methods for arriving at
the right decision.

de Bono, Edward   *Six Thinking Hats* (APTT 1992)
A splendid analysis of de Bono's famous technique.

Foster, Timothy   *101 Ways to Generate Great Ideas* (Kogan Page 1991)
No-nonsense, practical guide. Short and sweet.

Hanks, Kurt and Parry, Jay   *Wake Up Your Creative Genius* (Kauffman 1983)
Funny, interesting, accessible – another good
introduction to the field.

Shore, Sidney X,   *Invent!* (Crisp Publications 1999)
Develops the useful idea of 'constructive discontent'.
I liked it, but perhaps aimed more at the
entrepreneur, rather than not-for-profit professional.

Hurt, Floyd	*Rousing Creativity* (Crisp Publications 1999) Great if you need to facilitate a session. good on 'idea generation techniques such as brainstorming, nominal grouping, etc.
Gelatt, H.B. and C.	*Creative Decision Making* (Crisp Publications 1991) Helpful if you feel that you need to 'believe yourself creative'. Uses a principle called 'positive uncertainty', which I liked.
Caviglioli, O.; Harris, I. and Tindall, B.	*Thinking Skills and 'Eye' Q – Visual Tools for Raising Intelligence* (Network Educational Press 2002) Great for trainers, or workshop leaders. Fully investigates the role of visual intelligence and the role of sight in developing creativity.

Great thinkers

Bragg, Melvin	*On Giants' Shoulders* (Hodder & Stoughton 1998)
Koestler, Arthur	*The Sleepwalkers – a History of Man's Changing Vision of the Universe* (Arkana Penguin 1989)

Business decision making

Keenan, Kate	*The Management Guide To Solving Problems* (Ravette 1996)
Various authors	*Harvard Business Review on Breakthrough Thinking* (Harvard Business School Publishing 1999)
Peters, Tom	*Liberation Management* (Macmillan 1992)
Campbell, D.; Stonehouse, G. and Houson, B.	*Business Strategy* (Butterworth Heinemann 1999)
Buckingham, Marcus and Coffman, Curt	*First, Break All the Rules* (Simon and Schuster 1999)

The mind and brain

Russell, Peter	*The Brain Book* (Routledge 1979)
Carter, Rita	*Mapping the Mind* (Phoenix 2002)
Winston, Robert	*The Human Mind* (Bantam Press 2003)

Notes and references

(1) Hudson, Mike *Managing Without Profit* (DSC 2002)

(2) Carter, Rita *Mapping the Mind* (Orion/Phoenix 2002)

(3) In a BBC Radio 4 interview with John Bird, broadcast in April 2004

(4) Winston, Robert *The Human Mind* (Bantam Press 2003) pages 49–50. Professor Smith reports on the work of Canadian psychologist D.O. Hebb who first suggested the 'plastic brain'.

(5) Adair, John *Decision Making and Problem Solving* (CIPD 1997)

(6) Actually, this is probably an urban legend. I hope it is true, because it is such a wonderful illustration of the point – but I can't say for sure.

(7) Keswick Jencks, Maggie *A View from the Front Line*

(8) This illustration is taken from *Thinkertoys* by Michael Michalko (Ten Speed Press 1991)

(9) For more information see *What is Total Quality Control? The Japanese Way, Kaoru Ishikawa* (Prentice Hall 1985)

(10) Abrahams, Marc *The Ig Nobel Prizes* (Plume 2004)
More information regarding the prizes and past winners can be obtained from www.improb.com

(11) www.creativitypool.com. There are lots of creativity-focused websites on the Net. This is just one of them. A Google search will give you lots of interesting options.

(12) Sternberg, R.J.; Kaufman, J.C. and Pretz, J.E. *The Creativity Conundrum: A Propulsion Model of Creative Contributions* (Philadelphia, PA 2002)

(13) Von Oech, Roger *A Whack on the Side of the Head* (Thorsons 1990)

(14) Cialdini, Robert *Influence – The Psychology of Persuasion* (Quill/Morrow, 1993), page 274

(15) *The Harvard Business Review* (1998)

(16) Caviglioli, O.; Harris I. and Tindall B. *Thinking Skills* (Network Educational Press 2002)

(17) Eno, Brian *A Year with Swollen Appendices* (Faber and Faber 1996)

(18) http://www.pff.org/aspensummit/aspen2001/Fiorinaspeech.htm

(19) Source: BBC News 18 March 2004. Reported on http://news.bbc.co.uk

(20) Adair, John   *Decision Making and Problem Solving* (CIPD 1997)

(21) Lewin, K.   *Field Theory in Social Science* (Harper and Row 1951)

(22) Locke, John   'An Essay Concerning Human Understanding' (1690)

(23) Winston, Robert   *The Human Mind* (Bantam Press 2003) page 326. Case Western Reserve University School of Medicine Study

(24) Smith, George   *Asking Properly* (White Lion Press 1996) page 65

(25) In an interview with Melvyn Bragg in *On Giant's Shoulders* (Hodder & Stoughton 1998) page 17

(26) Kolb, D.A.   *Experiential Learning: Experience as the Source of Learning and Development* (Prentice Hall 1984)

(27) Karni, A. and Sagi, D.   *Nature* No. 365 (1993)

(28) Leonard, Dorothy and Straus, Susan   'Putting Your Company's Whole Brain to Work', *Harvard Business Review on Breakthrough Thinking* (1999)

(29) Alford, M.   *Charity Appeals, the Complete Guide to Success* (JM Dent & Sons 1992)

(30) Kotler and Andreasen   *Strategic Marketing for Non-profit Organisations* (Prentice Hall 1996) pages 418–419

(31) Richardson, Alan   *Mental Imagery* (Springer Publishing Company, Inc. 1969)

(32) Guide Dogs for the Blind Annual Review. Chair's Statement 2002

(33) Shore, S.   *Invent!* (Crisp Publications 1999)

(34) Amabile, T.A.   'How to Kill Creativity' *Harvard Business Review on Breakthrough Thinking* (1999)

(35) Handy, C.   *Understanding Voluntary Organisations* (Penguin 1990) pages 90–91